THE WORLD
ACCORDING TO
GROUCHO
MARX

THE WORLD
ACCORDING TO
GROUCHO
MARX

DAVID BROWN

MICHAEL O'MARA BOOKS LIMITED

First published in Great Britain in 2002 by
Michael O'Mara Books Limited
9 Lion Yard
Tremadoc Road
London SW4 7NQ

A CIP catalogue record for this book is available from
the British Library

ISBN 1-85479-130-3

1 3 5 7 9 10 8 6 4 2

Designed and typeset by Design 23

Printed and bound in Finland by WS Bookwell, Juva

CONTENTS

To the memory of
Groucho and to Jackum,
who knows why.

INTRODUCTION

Ernst Lubitsch, the great German-American film producer and director, said, 'Nobody should try to play comedy unless they have a circus going on inside.' It is only too clear that Chico Marx, Harpo Marx and especially Groucho Marx each had quite a circus going on inside.

Groucho was born Julius Henry Marx in New York in 1890. His parents were European Jewish immigrants who had then only quite recently arrived in the United States. The Marx boys' early experience of poverty towards the end of the nineteenth century would have been similar to that of many immigrant families in America at the time, yet the Marx family, together with grandparents and assorted relatives and friends, do not appear to have been a typical first-generation immigrant family. The extraordinary sense of fun and happiness that surrounded them at home, together with the excitement of life on the street in New York at the time, would have had considerable influence on producing that 'circus' within the Marx Brothers outfit.

It is indeed fortunate that luck drove Groucho into the world of show business. Luck, that is, combined with the ambitious impulses of his mother, the amazing Minnie Marx, who would later say about show business, 'Where else can people who don't know anything make so much money?'

Groucho's lack of respect for authority, his disregard for convention or formality, his refusal to behave properly, his unwillingness and even perhaps his inability to 'obey the rules' are all qualities that, luckily for Groucho, we admire and enjoy in someone in show business. If Groucho had become a bank clerk or indeed the chiropodist that, briefly, he had once aspired to be, it is unlikely that either his customers or his patients would have been so understanding or so readily amused.

While the Marx Brothers are principally well known in Britain for their films, including *Duck Soup*, *A Day at the Races* and *A Night at the Opera*, their formative years were spent travelling across America performing on stage in vaudeville and then on Broadway in New York. It was during this period that they practised and honed their act, perfecting the style for which they were to become so famous. The Marx Brothers hit the big time in 1924, their heyday was during the 1930s and 1940s, and their last film together was made in 1950. Yet for many years afterwards the films were reshown with continuing success, producing new generations of Marx Brothers' fans.

Improvisation and ad-libbing featured strongly throughout most of the Marx Brothers' films. Often quite noticeable, it was a source of amusement to the audience who could quite clearly see their comedy heroes enjoying the performance as much as the viewers themselves. Such was the extent of free-flowing humour, that one scriptwriter of a Marx Brothers' film reported that he once had to wait for a whole five minutes before he could hear one of his original lines in a scene.

Though the Marx Brothers had effectively broken up as an act by the 1950s, Groucho soon established himself as a solo performer. As well as being a star of stage and screen, he went on to become famous in America for his radio and television work, especially the quiz programme *You Bet Your Life*, which was first broadcast on radio, and subsequently ran on US television for nearly twelve years.

From his first professional engagement as one third of the Larong Trio at the age of fifteen to his triumphant one-man show at New York's Carnegie Hall in 1972, Groucho had a career in show business that lasted for almost seventy years. He was even still occasionally appearing on television in 1976 at the age of eighty-five. While there were sometimes quiet periods in his working life in the 1960s, there was a huge renaissance of interest in his life and work in his final years. He was made a Commandeur dans l'Ordre des Arts et des Lettres by the French Government, and in 1974 received a special Oscar at the Academy Awards.

He was also a gifted writer – the author of a stage play, two screenplays, seven books and more than a hundred articles and essays for newspapers and magazines. He was a prolific letter-writer to family, fellow writers and performers, friends and even enemies, or at least potential ones. Some of Groucho's letters contain marvellous examples of his own special, inventive genius.

From 'Time wounds all heels' to 'I've had a perfectly wonderful evening. But this wasn't it', and 'A man is as young as the woman he feels' or 'I don't care to belong to any club that will have me as a member', Groucho's mastery of the one-liner was truly extraordinary. His ability to use, misuse and twist the English language has resulted in a variety of sayings, bons mots and quotations that are still famous throughout the English-speaking world. Some of his lines have taken on such a life of their own that many people are totally unaware that they were originally said or written by Groucho.

There have a only been a handful of people thoughout history who are immediately recognized by their first names but Groucho certainly is a member of that select band – as to a lesser extent also are Harpo, Chico, Zeppo and Gummo. The mere mention of the word Groucho instantly conjures up his staccato, wisecracking voice and his physical idiosyncratic trademarks: the painted moustache, the cigar, the frock coat and, last but not least, the loping walk. Unique is a strong and often misused word, yet only an unreasonable person would argue against it being used to describe the Marx Brothers. Which other group of brothers has had such success, such an impact on our consciousness, in show business or indeed in *any* field of human endeavour?

Although some of the scenes and gags in the Marx Brothers films may sometimes seem a bit dated now, there are numerous examples of madcap surreal genius in most of them which are absolutely timeless. Indeed there are echoes of their talent in the work of many more recent writers and performers of comedy. While all comics of course have their own individual styles, it would be a churlish individual who could deny that Woody Allen, *The Goon Show*, *Morecambe and Wise*, *Monty Python* or, more recently, *The Fast Show* all owed something to the Marx Brothers.

Some famous comics, however funny they are on stage, are distinctly unfunny off it. For them it is only an act, a performance that is entirely separate from their daily life. This was far from the case with Groucho. He was as funny off stage as he was under the spotlight. He wanted to be funny and have fun all the time – and for most of the time he was successful, although in his private life Groucho was not a great success as a husband, nor was he always the world's best father.

Though the private lives of showbiz stars are often interesting to their public, such personal information is considerably less important than their work. What *is* important about Groucho is his extraordinary comic genius. The world was, and will continue to be, enriched, amused and uplifted by the life and work of Julius Henry Marx.

THE EARLY YEARS

On stage and on film Groucho always appeared to be the more senior of the Marx Brothers, and one could easily be forgiven for thinking that he was also the eldest. Yet of the three principal Marx Brothers, he was in fact the youngest.

Born Julius Henry Marx in New York City on 2 October 1890, Groucho's German-Jewish parents, Samuel and Minnie (née Schoenberg), lived in Manhattan's Yorkville district, which was then mostly inhabited by newly arrived German and East European immigrants. This was at a time when some 40 per cent of New York's population was foreign born.

> ‘I was born at a very early age. Before I had time to regret it, I was four-and-a-half years old. Now that we're on the subject of age, let's skip it.’

Samuel Marx (originally Simon Marrix) was actually French, having been born and raised in Alsace-Lorraine, which was ceded by France to Germany when he was only eleven years old. Samuel, who was to carry the nickname ‘Frenchy’ for the rest of his life, always considered himself to be French and not German. Leaving the country that had become Germany to start a new life in America did not appear to have been a difficult decision for Samuel. First there was the promise of the

'New Golden Land', but just as important was the fact that he feared being called up to join the German army.

Through working as a tailor's apprentice, Samuel had saved up enough money to pay for his passage to America and he finally landed in New York in November 1882 at the age of twenty-two. Despite never having finished his apprenticeship, Samuel soon noticed that there seemed to be quite a few tailors in New York called Marx, including two of his cousins. While his knowledge of tailoring may have been rather vague, he did know something about the business. So, rather ambitiously, he decided to set up shop, billing himself as 'Samuel Marx, Custom Tailor to the Men's Trade'.

From the beginning he took a somewhat cavalier attitude to his chosen trade; he considered such equipment as a measuring tape, for example, to be an inessential trifle. Among his customers (who became ex-customers since they never returned) Samuel soon became known as 'Misfit Sam'. In later years Groucho remarked that his father's clients could easily be recognized in the street, as they all walked 'with one trouser shorter than the other, one sleeve longer than the other or coat collars undecided where to rest.' However, Sam's ability to speak French, German and Yiddish, coupled with his dapper appearance and snappy dress sense, could always be put to good use and he took to travelling far and wide around New York in his search for unsuspecting new clients. On his free evenings Samuel Marx began earning some much needed extra money by giving dancing lessons to attractive young Jewish women, amongst whom was a nineteen-year-old blonde called Minnie, the daughter of Lafe and Fanny Schoenberg.

In the late 1870s Lafe, who was then in his fifties, together with his wife Fanny and their seven children, had left his native Germany to seek a new life in America. Until that point the Schoenberg family had spent most of their time travelling around the German countryside, with Lafe earning a living as an itinerant ventriloquist and magician, while Fanny accompanied him on the harp. Lafe's prowess as a magician seems to have been the equal of his future son-in-law's talent for tailoring. Years later Groucho was to say about Lafe that 'as a magician he toured Europe for fifty years in a covered wagon that carried his wife, innumerable children, together with his scenery, and a harp. He could just as easily have been a sewing machine agent for all the magic he knew. But he got by.'

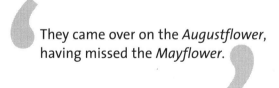

They came over on the *Augustflower*, having missed the *Mayflower*.

Settling in New York's East 10th Street, the Schoenbergs soon discovered that the city's streets were not paved with gold. Earning enough money to survive was tough. In Groucho's words, 'Since neither my grandfather nor my grandmother spoke any English, they were unable to get any theatrical dates in America. For some curious reason there seemed to be practically no demand for a German ventriloquist and a woman harpist who yodelled in a foreign language.' Lafe had to look elsewhere to earn a living and, quite bizarrely, decided that the umbrella repair business was the obvious choice. This was not a success, however, as in one year he made the princely sum of $12.50 from his new venture. Back to Groucho: 'Licking his wounds, Lafe decided to retire from the umbrella-mending business and embark on a new career. The new career consisted of never doing another day's work until he died, forty-nine years later.' So the responsibility for providing for the family was passed on to Minnie, her elder sister Hannah, and soon after by her brother Adolph.

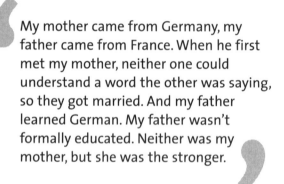

My mother came from Germany, my father came from France. When he first met my mother, neither one could understand a word the other was saying, so they got married. And my father learned German. My father wasn't formally educated. Neither was my mother, but she was the stronger.

Minnie took a job in the fur trade, working in one of New York's many sweatshops. She was a pretty, lively young woman with an hourglass figure, and first met the dashing young Samuel Marx at his dance lessons. A dazzling sight together on the dance floor, they were instantly attracted to each other. They were a good match too, as both of them were Jewish, recent immigrants from Western Europe and they both worked in the clothing trade. Minnie was clever and ambitious, and felt that the handsome young man before her had good prospects. Only later would she discover that Samuel was far more interested in playing the card game pinochle, chasing women and generally having a good time than he was in pursuing a career. But by that time it was too late – she was in love.

Lafe and Fanny Schoenberg clearly approved of their daughter's choice. So much so, in fact, that a couple of years later when Minnie and Samuel got married and set up house together, Lafe and Fanny moved in with them, together with several of their younger children.

> My mother was a great woman. She collected us, got us together. My mother gathered us together like you gather flowers. Can you imagine with all her struggles, she finally saw us become stars? Without her we would have been nothing.

Minnie and Samuel's first son, Manfred, was born in January 1886 but died of tuberculosis only six months later. Despite this early tragedy, they appeared to recover quickly: Leonard or Leo (later to become Chico) was born in March 1887, Adolph, later Arthur, (Harpo) in November the following year, Julius (Groucho) in October 1890 and Milton (Gummo) in October 1892. The youngest son, Herbert (Zeppo) was born nearly nine years later in February 1901.

Money was always in short supply for the Marx family in those early years. There were often rows with landlords over the rent, which resulted in frequent moves until they finally found an affordable three-room apartment on East 93rd Street, where they would stay for fifteen years. Apart from the five brothers and Samuel and Minnie, there was Lafe and Fanny and often one or more of their other children, not to mention an adopted sister Pauline (who was almost certainly the illegitimate daughter of Minnie's sister Hannah) and, according to Groucho, 'a steady stream of poor relations that flowed through our house night and day.'

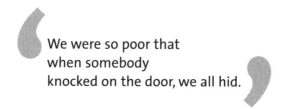

'We were so poor that when somebody knocked on the door, we all hid.'

Despite their ongoing financial problems, life with the Marx family was rarely unhappy. Neither Minnie nor Samuel were prone to moments of gloom or depression. They had a positive outlook and took life as it came. Their home was virtually open house to various relatives and friends. Visitors were always calling by for a chat and a coffee. Aside from his passion for pinochle, Samuel (who soon began to be called Frenchy, even by all of his sons) had a great interest in cooking. His culinary talent greatly surpassed his ability as a tailor. As Groucho said, 'It's amazing how proficient a man can be in one field and how incompetent in another. My father should have been a chef. He usually cooked dinner for all of us. He could take two eggs, some stale bread, a few assorted vegetables and a hunk of cheap meat, and convert this into something fit for the gods.'

Harpo was later to write about his father in his autobiography: 'Frenchy was a trim and handsome little man, with twinkling brown eyes and a face that was smoothly sculptured around a permanent thin-lipped smile…Throughout all the hungry, rugged days of my childhood, Frenchy never stopped working. He never ducked his responsibility of being the family breadwinner. He tried the best he could, at the job he stubbornly thought he could do the best. Frenchy was a loving, gentle man, who accepted everything that happened – good luck or tragedy – with the same unchangeable, sweet nature. He had no ambition beyond living and accepting life from day to day. He had only two vices: loyalty to everybody he ever knew (he never had an enemy, even among the sharpies who fleeced him), and the game of pinochle.'

Samuel's nickname was given to him not simply as a result of his nationality; as Groucho was to reminisce many years later, 'We called him Frenchy – partly because he could only speak French when he first came to this country from Alsace-Lorraine, and partly because of his passion for dancing, lively neckties and good cooking. I sat looking at my father at dinner the other night, when the entire family was gathered at my house. Frenchy was the most dapper man at the table; there was scarcely a wrinkle on his face, and his appetite was better than mine. We talked about things theatrical, and business conditions, but Frenchy was only mildly interested. He was wondering which of us boys would take him on for a game of pinochle.'

In complete contrast to her husband's cooking skills, Minnie was hopeless in the kitchen. In the beginning she would attempt the various chores associated with homemaking, but soon passed even these on to the uncomplaining Samuel. Minnie's talents – and they were many – lay elsewhere. As Groucho would recall in his autobiography, *Groucho and Me*, 'Whatever our visitors came for, they always came to my mother – never to my father. She advised them about their love-lives, where to find jobs and how to stay out of trouble. She engineered loans when they needed money. How she did it was always a source of wonder to me, but she invariably came through. She patched up marriages that were foundering and she out-talked the landlord, the grocer, the butcher and anyone else to whom we owed money. Her manoeuvres were a triumph of skill, chicanery and imagination.'

Harpo's idolization of his mother was as strong as Groucho's: 'A lot has been written about Minnie Marx. She's become a legend in show business. And just about everything anybody ever said about her is true. Minnie was quite a gal. She was a lovely woman, but her soft, doe-like looks were deceiving. She had the stamina of a brewery horse, the drive of a salmon fighting his way up a waterfall, the cunning of a fox, and a devotion to her brood as fierce as any she-lion's. Minnie loved to whoop it up. She liked to be in the thick of things, whenever there was singing, storytelling, or laughter.'

Minnie was a great organizer and extremely adept at using her considerable charm and feminine guile. She was smart, jolly and amusing and a great expert at the verbal put-down, a talent which would be inherited by her middle son, Groucho, and one for which he would become famous throughout the world. But perhaps more than anything else Minnie was ambitious. Soon realizing that her ambitions stood no chance of being realized by her beloved Samuel, her focus shifted to her five sons. Not only was Minnie the creator (or, more accurately, the co-creator) of the Marx brothers she can also, more than anyone else, be credited as the creator of the Marx Brothers.

Groucho was different from the other Marx boys from the beginning. Both Chico and Harpo were chunky babies and blond like Minnie. Groucho did not have Minnie's fair skin, nor did he have Samuel's neat rather distinguished features. Groucho had a slightly swarthy complexion with dark, curly hair, a big nose and, most noticeably, a wandering eye – the moustache, the cigar and the frock-coat were all to come later!

Chico always remained Minnie's favourite son. A naughty boy, he was given a lot of leeway at home and could get away with almost anything. He had also inherited Minnie's beguiling charm, which he was able to turn on at will to persuade friends, strangers and, later, women and then, even later, audiences to fall in love with him.

Neither Chico nor Harpo were a great success at school. Though Chico was clearly an intelligent boy (Groucho said that he 'had a brain as fast and accurate as a calculating machine'), from an early age he showed a natural aptitude for mathematics and could work out quite complicated arithmetic in his head, but he was unable to concentrate at school for any length of time and much preferred having a good time and general mischief-making. He was quickly able to put his mathematical abilities to good use, however, as a successful street corner gambler. According to his daughter Maxine, he was already a compulsive gambler by the age of nine. Chico was bored with all the lessons and after constantly nagging at his parents to let him leave school, Minnie and Samuel finally agreed. Chico's experience of the world of formal education was thus to end when he was just thirteen years old.

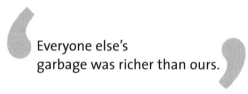

Everyone else's
garbage was richer than ours.

Harpo's time at school was, if anything, even worse. As he was later to write in his autobiography *Harpo Speaks!*, 'I never had much schooling. The sad fact is, I never even finished the second grade... How I came to be educated, over the years, I don't exactly know. I only know that it didn't happen during my sojourn at New York City Public School No. 86.'

His attitude to school was not exactly favourable: 'School was all wrong. It didn't teach anybody how to exist from day to day, which was how the poor had to live. School prepared you for Life – that thing in the far-off future – but not for the World, the thing you had to face today, tonight, and when you woke in the morning with no idea of what the new day would bring...'

In comparison with his two older brothers' experience, Groucho's period at school was considerably more successful. Though by no means a scholar and while he often found school difficult, he did at least try hard – for the first few years anyway – and was especially interested in history and science. Groucho was in many ways the classic middle child. The oldest two boys and the youngest two formed natural pairs. Chico and Harpo had their own private jokes, games and secrets and were usually to be seen together, generally playing around and being naughty. Groucho was a more withdrawn child and more of a loner. He became an avid reader and would devour the many pulp novels and magazines of the time. He was especially drawn to real-life adventure stories and tales of derring-do. He was envious of Chico and Harpo's closeness, and their sense of fun and mischief. Indeed Minnie would sometimes refer to Groucho as 'der Eifersuchtige', or 'the jealous one'.

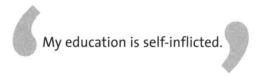

My education is self-inflicted.

Though Groucho had shown early promise at school, he too soon became restless and impatient to find his way in the big wide world. When he looked back on his school days, Groucho seems to have become almost as disenchanted with formal education as Harpo: 'School was an unspeakable bore, and the only thing that interested me was the teacher, a tall, shapely blue-eyed Irish girl… The rest of my studies seemed pretty useless. algebra and geometry were tools of the devil, devised to make life miserable for small, stupid boys.'

In their later years, when writing and talking about their childhood and adolescence, the brothers would often be rather vague about when events actually took place. Sometimes dates were moved forward or back a couple of years, ages were overstated or understated, and often their accounts of the events themselves were exaggerated or dressed up. Perhaps they had merely forgotten the details or maybe the inaccuracy was deliberate to spice up the truth.

> We slept four in a bed, two at each end. There were ten of us and one toilet. That I call pretty poor, but we didn't know it. We were happy. We loved our mother and father.

So although Harpo definitely left school at a young age, his claim to have left at the age of only eight may have been somewhat exaggerated. In fact Harpo was expelled from school, though it was a rather more literal expulsion than normal. Harpo, the only Jewish boy in the class, was rather small for his age and had a rather squeaky voice. There were two Irish boys in the class who used to make a habit of picking on him and often, while the teacher was out of the room for any reason, they would heave Harpo out of the schoolroom window. There was an eight-foot drop to the ground so little Harpo would land shaken and angry, but without any bones broken. He refused to tell his teacher, a certain Miss Flatto, who would then punish him for leaving the class without her permission. One day, when Harpo had been thrown out of the window for the umpteenth time, he picked himself up and walked home, never to return to school again.

> The two sisters (Minnie and Hannah) were inseparable. They were so lovely. They always wore big hats, and they were poor, but they always looked so attractive in those hats and pretty dresses. Minnie Marx was a fascinating woman – good-looking and always jolly. That woman was really something. Those boys owed everything to Minnie Marx. Except Groucho. He would have made it on his own.

ETHEL WISE (THE MARX FAMILY'S NEIGHBOUR ON EAST 93RD STREET)

After much nagging at his parents, Groucho also left school at the age of fourteen. As his pocket money at the time was only five cents a week, Groucho set off on an urgent search for work. He scoured the wanted ads in the newspaper and spied a vacancy for an office boy at a nearby estate agents. He got the job, which paid $3.50 a week, but it proved to be rather undemanding work. The sum total of his responsibilities was opening the letters and answering the phone. Since the only mail the firm received was advertising circulars and nobody ever rang, Groucho soon became bored with his first foray into the big wide world of employment: 'Having nothing better to do, I spent most of the mornings eating grapes and spitting seeds on the carpet. The afternoons I spent picking up the seeds... It certainly was quiet in that office. It was like living in a mausoleum with a carpet.' Since his boss seemed to arrive at the office very late and leave very early, Groucho took to doing the same, though making sure that he was always there just before and just after the boss. It seemed to be a pretty safe system until one day when he was strolling about in the local park, he caught a man's hat that had blown off in the wind. He returned the hat to its owner who turned out to be... the boss. Groucho was fired. It was not a good start to his working life.

For a brief while he returned to school but he soon began to get itchy feet, growing desperate to make his way in the world.

TREADING THE BOARDS

One of the regular visitors to the Marx family home was Minnie's brother, 'Uncle Al'. Al Shean, whose real name was Abraham Elieser Adolph Schoenberg, had started to work on the stage in 1888, two years before Groucho's birth. Al's early jobs had been as a butcher's boy, a messenger and then as a tailor's apprentice and trouser presser, but he had always had a yearning for the theatre. After all he would be continuing the family tradition set by his father Lafe, the itinerant magician. Al's wish to follow in his father's footsteps into the entertainment world may have had its origins in the memories of his early childhood spent travelling around the German countryside while his parents performed.

Legend has it that Al used to sing in his fine baritone voice to entertain his fellow workers in the trouser-pressing business, but what is known for sure is that his first professional engagement was as one of the 'Manhattan Quartet' performing in a variety theatre on New York's 14th Street. His first hit show was a rural drama called *The Country Fair* which ran for over three years. Al's role, which required him to ride a horse onstage at one point as well as sing, earned him more than thirty dollars a week, a tidy sum at the time especially compared with the Marx family's average weekly income.

The 1890s was the heyday of vaudeville and the 'Manhattan Comedy Four', as they were soon renamed, began to be noticed in a big way. They toured America and their act was well received everywhere. Al's salary quickly rose to $250 a week, more than ten times his earnings for a sixty-hour week as a trouser presser. In addition to performing as part of the foursome, Al began to write sketches, not only for their own act but also for some of the other groups with whom they toured. So confident was Al of his future prospects that in 1900 he left the 'Manhattan Comedy Four' to pursue a solo career. His confidence proved to be well founded, for Al Shean went on to a successful stage career which lasted many years. The highpoint was probably his partnership with Ed Gallagher in the Ziegfeld Follies in 1922, which produced the famous catchphrase 'Absolutely, Mr Gallagher; Positively, Mr Shean'.

> What Henry the Eighth was to English history and Torquemada was to the Spanish Inquisition, the theatre manager was to vaudeville.

Not surprisingly, Uncle Al's visits to the Marx home as the boys were growing up were to make a lasting impression on them, for not only would he turn up expensively dressed – complete with silk hat, gold cane, spats and fancy jewellery – but he would also give them a dollar each, as well as passing out coins to all the local children on the street. His role in the story of the start of the Marx Brothers was crucial, almost as important as that of their mother's. For while it was Minnie who provided the ambition that was virtually to force them into show business, it was Al who provided the experience.

Groucho's seemingly inauspicious introduction as a performer was on Coney Island in New York City, where he 'sang on a beer keg and made a dollar'. Soon after, Minnie, impressed with Groucho's soprano singing voice, encouraged him to join the choir at an Episcopalian church on Madison Avenue. The very idea of a fifteen-year-old Groucho Marx dressed in a white surplice, singing Christian hymns in a church in a high voice, may seem incredible, if not surreal, or even a scene featuring in an unknown Marx Brothers' movie.

Groucho's first 'proper' job in show business came as a result of an advertisement which read: BOY SINGER WANTED FOR STAR VAUDEVILLE ACT. ROOM AND BOARD AND FOUR DOLLARS A WEEK. Scared that thousands of other boys would be applying and that he would be too late, Groucho ran all the way to the audition, rushed up five flights of stairs of the dingy tenement block and knocked on the door. He was greeted by a middle-aged man in full make-up, wearing a kimono. The gentleman, whose name was Robin Larong, announced to Groucho that he had just begun the auditioning session up on the roof, where more than thirty hopeful young boys were assembled. Amazingly, Groucho got the job; another boy called Johnny Morris was also taken on as a dancer. Groucho was on his way. As he was later to recall in his autobiography, 'I felt for the first time in my life I wasn't a nonentity. I was part of the Larong Trio. I was an actor. My dream had come true.'

As things unfolded, the fulfilment of Groucho's dream was not quite complete. The national tour of the Larong Trio that he was expecting turned out to involve performances in just two towns – Grand Rapids in Michigan and that other great metropolis, Cripple Creek in Colorado. Furthermore, the act itself was rather different, and its reception somewhat less enthusiastic, from Groucho's expectations, as he would later remember, 'We opened with the three of us dressed in short skirts, silk stockings, high-heeled shoes and large, floppy Merry Widow hats… Then, donning an altar boy's outfit, I reappeared and sang "Jerusalem, lift up your gates and sing" to a houseful of silence. The only one who applauded was a religious fanatic who…stood up on his seat and shouted, "Hallelujah!".'

Offstage, Groucho was also having little luck. After the final show in Cripple Creek, on his return to the boarding house where the trio were staying, Groucho discovered that the flighty Robin Larong had indeed flown, taking young Johnny Morris with him and stealing all Groucho's money, the hard-earned $8 from this, his debut engagement. After more trials and tribulations, Groucho eventually found his way back to New York and home. He was not downhearted, though he did then spend a short time doing what is known in the acting profession as 'resting'. At this point Minnie came into her own, descending upon New York's agents, attempting to persuade them that what they really needed was a juvenile boy singer. Eventually she was successful and Groucho was taken on to assist in the act of a glamorous English singer called Lillian Foster.

Miss Foster, a 'born and bred Yorkshire lass' who specialized in impersonations of London costermongers' songs, had been hired to join the bill of a vaudeville tour of Texas. Sharing the bill with her and Groucho were a group of clog dancers, a seventy-four-year-old tenor singer, plus a group of African lions, complete with lion tamer. After two weeks of rehearsals with Lillian, Groucho realized that there was some good news and some bad news about his latest foray into show business. The good news was that he found Lillian enormously sexy and was very attracted to her; the bad news was that she had even less talent in the singing department than he did.

> My advice to all young men is to start chasing girls the day you start tying your own shoelaces.

The tour, however, encompassing such places as Dallas, Houston and Hot Springs, must have given Groucho some valuable and much needed experience of performing in front of an audience. He also received his first reviews in the local press – the *San Antonio Light* and the *Waco Gazette*. Though the reviews were far from positive, they did actually mention his name. It is thus unfortunate that Groucho's second vaudeville tour, though considerably longer than his first, came to a sudden and rather abrupt end when the glamorous Lillian ran off with the lion tamer. And once again, despite the fact that Groucho had been trying to keep his money safely in his 'grouch bag' – a chamois leather bag worn round the neck – his earnings had disappeared with her.

In some accounts of this period in Groucho's life, the English singer's name is given as Lily Seville, not Lillian

Foster, but perhaps more interesting is the fact that these accounts state that the lion tamer, far from being the tall swarthy Neapolitan known as Professor Renaldo in Groucho's own version of the story, was actually a woman by the name of Martha Florrine. Following his poor treatment at the hands of Robin Larong, perhaps revealing the loss of his 'leading lady' to another woman was too much to admit for Groucho.

Groucho's salary on tour had been $15 a week, but after Miss Foster's unexpected departure, he was now back with Minnie and Samuel in New York, 'resting' once more. This time, thanks to Minnie's hustling round the New York agents, Groucho secured an opening in a firm of wigmakers at the distinctly less appealing salary of $3 a week. As it is well known, however, Groucho's destiny was not to be a wigmaker, and he left the job after seven weeks.

Budding impresario Gus Edwards was then building a reputation for his nurturing of the performing talents of young hopefuls; other stars who were to benefit from his tuition included Eddie Cantor and Eleanor Powell. In the spring of 1906 Groucho joined the seven other boys and one girl in 'Gus Edwards' Postal Telegraph Boys'. Their first performance, at New York's Alhambra Theatre, took place on 28 April, just ten days after the San Francisco earthquake. To raise money for victims of the earthquake, the Telegraph Boys performed at numerous fashionable restaurants in New York and were also given a spot on the all-day earthquake benefit show at the Metropolitan Opera House in front of an audience of 3,000 people. Groucho sang a solo piece, 'Somebody's Sweetheart I Want to Be', accompanied by a seventy-piece orchestra, which drew cheers from the packed house – it was Groucho's first taste of the big time.

When you're onstage, that's all you're thinking about... I was never nervous because I knew I was better than the audience. You have to feel that way or you can't get up there and do what you have to do.

Groucho stayed with Gus Edwards, performing with members of his often hastily assembled troupes and casts, for more than a year. He went on a tour with the play *Man Of Her Choice,* which was to take him to many towns in the eastern United States and Canada throughout the winter of 1906-7. The *New York Dramatic Mirror* reported that, 'Julius Marx made quite a hit in a "kid" part', and Groucho gained more useful experience of treading the boards. It was also during this tour that Groucho lost his virginity, with unpleasant consequences: he slept with a prostitute in Montreal, only to discover a day or two later that he had caught gonorrhoea.

All this time, while Groucho was learning his acting skills, Chico and Harpo were still at the family home in New York but they had been busy too, in their own ways. Since leaving school Chico had done a variety of dead-end jobs but he would always squander any money he earned on illegal street-corner gambling. He was also in the habit of taking the clothes that Samuel had made for clients to the local pawnshop to raise the money to pay off gambling debts. It is a tribute to Minnie's powers of persuasion, therefore, that for some years now Chico had been taking piano lessons – paid for by Minnie, of course. He had proved himself rather good at 'tinkling the ivory', so much so in fact that he had even begun to get occasional jobs as house pianist at a number of low-life honky-tonk bars in New York.

Harpo, who still bore a remarkable resemblance to his elder brother and at the time was working as a trainee butcher, had picked up the basics of piano-playing from him, which was to prove rather handy to the rather cunning Chico. For, after a while, when Chico was being offered more dates than he could manage, he came up with the idea that he could do two jobs in the same evening simply by getting Harpo to perform one of the dates in his place, as though he was Chico. The ruse was a success for quite a while, and even when they were found out, they simply moved to the bars in another neighbourhood. It appears that both Chico and Harpo had a rather limited repertoire – 'Love Me and the World is Mine' and 'Waltz Me Around Again, Willie', as well as a few other classics of the time.

The next person the indomitable Minnie targeted was Gus Edwards's colleague, Edward Wayburn. This proved to be a shrewd move, for Wayburn's career as a producer/impresario was to outlast that of Edwards by far. Wayburn was very aware that children's acts were good box-office earners at the time and he soon agreed to take on not only Groucho but also his totally inexperienced younger brother, Gummo. As Groucho was to put it later, 'Gummo, of all people! He had about as much equipment for the stage as the average Zulu has for psychiatry.'

Wayburn put Groucho and Gummo together with a sixteen-year-old girl called Mabel O'Donnell who had a strong – if not terribly tuneful – soprano singing voice. The resulting trio set off on a fairly extensive tour, with appearances in many cities and towns of the eastern states. Then, in November 1907, Wayburn stepped aside and Minnie decided to assume the trio's managerial mantel herself. Her first move was to sack Mabel O'Donnell and replace her with a boy singer called Lou Levy. This did not go down at all well with poor Mabel for, apart from anything else, she had developed quite a crush on Groucho. At the same time Minnie came up with the name for the trio – The Three Nightingales. As Groucho said later, 'There are three logical reasons why she could have called us The Three Nightingales. One, she had never heard a nightingale. Two, she was tone deaf. Three, she had a great sense of humour.'

> At that time, the actor's position in society was somewhere between that of a gypsy fortune teller and a pickpocket.

Minnie was soon successful in securing a debut appearance for her trio at a theatre in Coney Island. However just hours before the curtain was due to go up on their first night, she discovered that the theatre had been promoting the act in advance as a quartet. Nothing daunted, Minnie had – within half an hour – dragooned nineteen-year-old Harpo to step in to fill this unexpected vacancy, in a bass singing role. Thus were The Four Nightingales born.

It may seem hard to believe but The Four Nightingales apparently received wild applause from the audience at the opening night and the review in *Variety* praised their 'high degree of excellence'. So, encouraged by this early acclaim, Minnie set about organizing an extensive tour for the boys. She even managed to cajole her husband to get involved, presumably because there was an even greater dearth of customers for Frenchy's ill-cut clothes than usual. His role was to buy the train and bus tickets, and book the boarding-houses for the tour. Moreover, if customers were ever a bit slow to show their appreciation of the four aspiring stars, Frenchy could be relied upon to start cheering or clapping at the appropriate moment from a prominent position in the audience.

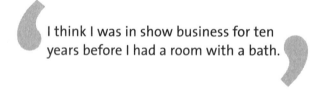

I think I was in show business for ten years before I had a room with a bath.

It was during this tour that the boys' act began to develop, mostly at Groucho's instigation. Until then The Four Nightingales had been a strictly singing act; Minnie felt strongly that any comedy diversions would not be appreciated by their audiences and were therefore out of order. However, Groucho started to add impromptu gags and little bits of business to their routine, which seemed to go down well – the audiences laughed. It was one of the rare instances when Minnie's instincts were wrong, though for the next few years she would still sometimes shout the word, 'Greenbaum', her codeword for 'stop', from the side of the stage, if she felt that the comic business onstage was getting out of hand.

At the end of the tour they returned to New York, but were surprised to find that securing bookings there proved difficult, and even Minnie's powers of persuasion were failing to have any effect on the agents. Things looked bleak but Minnie was not prepared to give up on her sons. Knowing that three of the biggest vaudeville circuits were centred on Chicago, Minnie resolved that they would relocate in their search for new pastures. Despite the fact that vaudeville throughout America was experiencing tough times, with taxes on theatres on the increase and all live performers were suffering as a result of the success of a new type of entertainment, the silent movie, the entire Marx household moved to Chicago.

> Theatrically, we were at the bottom of the social ladder. Five performances a day in a ten-cent vaudeville theatre was about as low as you could get.

Having borrowed $1,000 from brother Al, Minnie used the money as a down-payment on the purchase of a three-storey brownstone house in a Jewish section of Chicago. Such was her confidence in the Marx family's future prospects, she even employed the services of a housemaid who, as it transpired, would spend most of her time resisting the amorous advances of Grandpa Lafe, the strapping eighty-seven-year-old.

Minnie soon took steps to reorganize the boys' act. She replaced Lou Levy with another young man to be a bass singer and took on two girl dancers. So The Four Nightingales were replaced by 'The Six Mascots'. But the act was not a success in its new incarnation, and the two girl dancers soon left. Minnie's next inspiration was the decision to replace the two girls by herself, then a rather buxom fifty-year-old, and her sister Hannah, an even more buxom fifty-five-year-old. As Groucho later recorded, 'The fact that neither my mother nor her sister had the slightest talent didn't bother my mother in the least. She said she knew many people in show business who didn't have any talent. At that moment she was looking at me.'

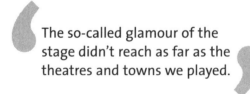

The so-called glamour of the stage didn't reach as far as the theatres and towns we played.

When Groucho asked Minnie what roles she and her sister were going to play in the act, she replied, 'Hannah and I will sing "Two Little Girls in Blue" as a duet. We'll pretend we're schoolgirls. We'll dress real young, in blue dresses, and the audience will think we're two little girls. I'm sure they'll love it.' Not surprisingly, things did not quite turn out exactly as Minnie had intended. On their first – and what was also to be their last – performance, having decided to remove their spectacles in order to appear more girlish, Minnie and Hannah were barely able to find their way onto the stage, and when they did, they attempted to sit on the same chair which promptly broke into several pieces under their substantial combined weight. The accompanying pianist instantly broke into playing 'The Star-Spangled Banner' as Minnie and Hannah, now in a bit of a panic, groped their way offstage. The Six Mascots had had a short life, albeit an interesting one. So, as if by magic, The Four Nightingales were reborn.

At this time, the comedy in the act began to come to the fore. While they continued to perform a few songs, these were now mostly of the send-up variety. Groucho, then in his early twenties, had been gaining in confidence as a performer, as had Harpo and Gummo. They had started to feel relaxed on stage, a place where they could have fun and make up jokes both with and against each other. They began to enjoy themselves and so did the audiences. Word of mouth was attracting new and enthusiastic crowds and the reviews in the press were getting better all the time. Groucho had begun to invent and write sketches which brought some of the biggest laughs in the show. The Four Nightingales name was now no longer appropriate. In truth, it probably never was appropriate but, since the comic routines were now the mainstay of the performance, it was now completely misleading and irrelevant. So Groucho came up with a new name for the act. It was honest, straightforward and it had a pleasing familiar ring to it. It was 'The Marx Brothers'.

Despite his own busy schedule, Uncle Al started to help by writing some of the sketches for his nephews' show and assisting Groucho with the rewriting of a school sketch, called 'Fun in Hi Skule!', that they had been performing for a while. In the sketch Groucho played the teacher, wearing a wig that made him look bald; Gummo was a young 'Hebrew boy' with a Yiddish accent; and Harpo, in a mad-looking red wig, was a half-Irish village idiot called Patsy Brannigan. After some encouragement from his brothers, Chico was persuaded to join the act around this time and his presence gave the act an extra sparkle. Chico had a great sense of timing onstage and he decided to acquire a rather extravagant Italian accent, which he had copied from his favourite New York barber. He proved a great hit with the audiences and, just as important for Groucho, with the chorus girls in the show. Girls would fall for Chico's charms and Groucho would sometimes have success with one of his cast-offs, which was much appreciated by Groucho for, until then, most of his sexual experiences appear to have been paid ones with hotel chambermaids.

> We were always in hookshops. We were the hit of the hookshops. It was the only place you could get laid in a strange town. They didn't want any actors. In a lot of towns they used to hide their daughters... In those days, the hookers used to come to the shows, and if they liked your act, they would send you a note backstage that you could come and visit 'em if you wanted to. So we were a big hit in those places. Harpo and Chico both played the piano, and I sang.

The Four Marx Brothers then embarked on a gruelling tour, often performing thirty shows a week in towns throughout the southern and mid-western states. They took the latest show to one of Chicago's most important venues but, much to the boys' disappointment, the reaction from audiences and the press was only lukewarm at best. Once again Uncle Al came to the rescue. He advised that their stage characters needed to be more structured: Groucho to have the main speaking role, Chico as the mischievous Italian, Gummo as the rather straight, smiling juvenile and Harpo as the crazy one with hardly any lines at all. They all concurred, even Harpo once he had got them to agree that he could make up for his absence of lines by doing a lot of ad-libbing onstage. The new show, now called *Home Again*, went on tour and seemed to work. As a result of one Illinois reviewer's comments, Harpo decided to dispense with his lines altogether and instead, to firm up his stage character, he acquired a grubby raincoat and an old car foghorn to honk out his replies. Harpo never spoke in performance again.

It was also around this time that the brothers acquired the nicknames by which they became known around the world. Sharing the bill with them on their latest tour was a stand-up comic called Art Fisher. One afternoon between shows, when they were all playing a game of poker together, Art Fisher told them that they would never become really big stars while they were called Julius, Leonard, Adolph and Milton. So he suggested that Leonard become Chico on account of his affinity for 'chicks', Milton become Gummo because he always put on gumshoes at the first sign of rain and Adolph become

Harpo because of his tremendous enthusiasm for playing his late grandmother Fanny's harp. Julius was to become Groucho because of the grouch bag in which he liked to keep his money – though some people think it was possibly because he could from time to time be grouchy in manner. It would appear that Mr Fisher never received a penny for his very important piece of advice, nor does history record who won the poker game.

> We Marx Brothers never denied our Jewishness. We simply didn't use it. We could have safely fallen back on the Yiddish theatre, making secure careers for ourselves. But our act was designed from the start to have a broad appeal. If, because of Chico, a segment of the audience thought we were Italian, then let them...

As they became more successful, the Marx Brothers gained in confidence onstage and off. Ever since Chico had joined the act, the larking about onstage had increased and soon they discovered that life could be more fun if they larked about offstage as well. While Chico would usually stick to his low-life gambling joints, Groucho and Harpo started to play pranks and all manner of practical jokes on the chorus girls, other fellow performers and theatre managers, not to mention the staff of sundry boarding houses and restaurants. They realized they could get away with it – though there were occasional run-ins with outraged fathers and husbands, who did not always see the joke. Occasionally they would get their comeuppance too, like the time when a particularly irritated theatre manager paid them their $120 fee in single cent pieces just before they had to rush off to the railway station.

> We played towns I would refuse
> to be buried in today, even if the
> funeral were free and
> they tossed in a tombstone.

The year 1914 had seen the beginning of the First World War in Europe and in May the following year the *Lusitania*, carrying supplies to Britain, was torpedoed by German submarines causing the deaths of more than one thousand people, including many Americans. The atmosphere in America changed overnight. Any German accents in the Marx Brothers show suddenly became Dutch and allusions to things German in the sketches had to be altered. Worse still, conscription loomed. On learning that people involved in agriculture were exempt from the draft, Minnie acted with admirable foresight and bought a farm. Unlikely as it may seem, the Marx Brothers for a period then became farmers, of a sort, on a twenty-seven-acre homestead in La Grange, Illinois, a couple of stops on the train from Chicago. However, the Marx family's aptitude for first raising chickens and then breeding guinea pigs (Zeppo had got the idea that guinea pigs were much in demand by medical laboratories, when in fact it was rabbits that were required) proved to be on a par with Groucho's talent as a wigmaker.

At some stage in 1917, the draft board finally caught up with the brothers. As luck would have it, apart from Gummo, they were all rejected: Groucho on account of his poor eyesight, Harpo had bad kidneys, Chico was too old and Zeppo was too young. Thus Gummo left to join the army, but without any regret, as he confessed that he hated the stage. He had always had stage-fright, not to mention a stammer, and he hated touring. His brothers were relieved at Gummo's departure because they had always felt his contribution to the show was somewhat lacking. Furthermore, they had an instant replacement ready to take over as their straight man – young Zeppo.

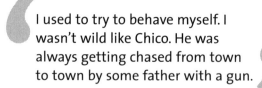

I used to try to behave myself. I wasn't wild like Chico. He was always getting chased from town to town by some father with a gun.

After their failure at animal husbandry, the Marx Brothers returned to their traditional pursuit and the *Home Again* show went back on the road. Groucho dumped the Yiddish accent that he had used onstage and took to using a cigar in order to punctuate the punchlines as well as inventing his loping walk. Chico had recently married Betty Karp, a pretty nineteen-year-old Jewish girl, and she joined the cast, mostly to put a damper on Chico's womanizing. She soon discovered that sharing the stage with the Marx Brothers was far from easy; Chico, her husband after all, in his very public assessment of her abilities, said to her, 'Baby, with your looks and your legs, if you had any talent, you'd be worth a million dollars.'

After a period back at the farm for the brothers, their Uncle Al carried out some major re-writing of the *Home Again* show, renamed it *'N'Everything* and the brothers went back on the road again. Audiences were even bigger and more appreciative than before. In his review of the show, the critic for the *Louisville Herald* said of the brothers' performances, 'Arthur Marx (Harpo) … never says a word, but as a comedian, he is an artist… Leonard Marx (Chico) as an Italian, boobs the part and is a splendid piano player. Herbert Marx (Zeppo) takes the part of a 'sissy son'… The dancing is done by Julius Marx (Groucho), who is surprisingly agile…'

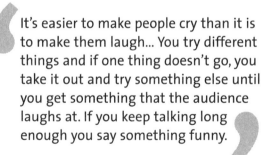

It's easier to make people cry than it is to make them laugh... You try different things and if one thing doesn't go, you take it out and try something else until you get something that the audience laughs at. If you keep talking long enough you say something funny.

In February 1920, their remarkable grandpa, Lafe, the retired ventriloquist and magician, finally died at the age of ninety-seven – though Groucho was later to claim that he was 101. It was the end of an era in the Marx Brothers' life in another way too, for the touring vaudeville show as a popular art form was fast losing popularity. People now thought it old-fashioned and were deserting it in ever increasing numbers for that new medium, the cinema. For the Marx Brothers, however, the news was not so devastating, as they had all become tired of the touring, the one-night stands, and the tawdry boarding houses they were obliged to stay in while on the road.

In the same month, thirty-year-old Groucho married Ruth Johnson, a dancer whom Zeppo had hired in Cleveland, Ohio, during the *Home Again* tour.

> I always had a hunger to read. I used to sit in my dressing room and read. I left the door open so the other actors would think I was educated. I always wanted more education, but now my books are in the Library of Congress.

By the end of 1920 all five brothers were back in New York City again, but this time living in separate apartments. With Chico having effectively replaced Minnie as manager, the Marx Brothers set about conquering the 'Big Apple'. Their first venture was in fact to embark upon a tour with a difference: all the venues were in and around New York, so they were mostly able to return home at the end of each show. The tour lasted for the next fourteen months. By the end of it, they felt they were ready for a new challenge – a big production with first-class script, proper scenery and a large cast.

This soon came in the shape of a musical comedy set in a theatrical manager's office called *On the Mezzanine* (later called *On the Balcony*) written by the writer and composer Herman Timberg, who was known in show business as 'the pint-sized humorist'. The show was a hit and proceeded to earn the brothers around $2,800 a week for the next two years – a sum that they had previously only dreamed about. Their co-star in the show was Timberg's sister Hattie Darling who later recalled, 'They took me out to dinner. They took me all over. The best notice I ever received was with the Marx Brothers in *On the Mezzanine*. They were wonderful to me. And Groucho had a sense of humour I have never seen in anybody else.'

During the New York tour Groucho became a father for the first time, with the birth of his son, Arthur, in July 1921.

At the end of this successful run, they made the daring decision to take the show in an adapted and shortened form to England. It opened at the London Coliseum on 19 June 1922, and sharing the bill were comedian Tommy Handley, Mademoiselle Ninette de Valois, a Russian dance company, and a lady called Cecilia Loftus, who was famous for her apparently excellent imitations of famous theatre people at the time – from Sarah Bernhardt and Marie Lloyd to Sir Harry Lauder. Although some of the reviews for the brothers' British debut were not too bad, the audiences hated them. As Harpo said later, 'People began to hoot and whistle and throw pennies at us… We had never been so humiliated in public in all our professional lives.' It is possible that most of the audience had come to see the Russian dancers or Tommy Handley, but more likely that the Marx Brothers' humour failed to click with a London audience at that time. Within four days they had dropped *On the Balcony* and replaced it with that old faithful *Home Again*, but this also received a poor reception. *The Times* wrote scathingly that they 'so obviously enjoy their own performance that it cannot be long before they persuade their audiences to do the same.'

The show transferred to London's Alhambra Theatre and then toured to Manchester and Liverpool where things got a little better, but not much. It seems quite remarkable that Harpo was able to remember anything good about the experience: 'We found that the English everywhere gave actors and vaudevillians special treatment... Here was genuine kindness and dignity in show business – even between the most eminent impresarios and the seediest performers.' However it must surely have been an unhappy time for the brothers and they were back in America before the end of July. They did not return to Britain for nearly ten years, by which time they were stars of Hollywood.

Things were far from easy on their return to New York. They had seriously angered Edward Albee, the 'Mr Big' of theatre and vaudeville at the time, by going to England without getting his permission first, and they were therefore barred from appearing in a large number of venues for a while. They embarked on a tour of different venues controlled by a rival chain with a show called the *Twentieth Century Review*, but although the press reviews were better than ever, they could not attract big enough audiences. Losses mounted and the tour was brought to an abrupt end in Indianapolis when the vaudeville circuit company went bankrupt and the sheriff arrived backstage to gather up the costumes and scenery to sell off to pay local bills.

It was back to New York again, but there was no show, and no work in the offing. For quite a while their prospects looked grim, so much so that Minnie suggested that perhaps the time had come for the brothers to split and go their separate ways. Eventually, though, a combination of Chico's guile and gambling instinct coupled with several pieces of startlingly good luck resulted in a script for a major new show, a theatre to stage it in and, most important, enough cash with which to produce it. With this latest show, to be called *I'll Say She Is*, the Marx Brothers would finally hit the big time.

I'll Say She Is premiered in Philadelphia and played there to packed houses for three months. After successful runs in Chicago, Kansas City and Buffalo, the Marx Brothers were ready for their all-important opening night on 19 May 1924 in New York. The day before the opening night at Broadway's Casino Theatre they had another great stroke of luck. A show that all the main New York critics, including the most powerful and influential of them, Alexander Woollcott, had been due to attend on the same night was cancelled at the last minute. That night the Marx Brothers were clearly on sparkling form and their ad-libbing was at its most crazy and inventive. The audience roared their approval. The reviews the next morning, including Woollcott's, under the headline 'Hilarious Antics Spread Good Cheer at the Casino', were wonderful. The Marx Brothers had made it at last. And Minnie had been there in the front row to see it all, albeit with a broken leg. It was, as Groucho said, 'her personal victory...the culmination of twenty years of scheming, starving, cajoling and scrambling.'

I'll Say She Is ran to record houses in New York and it

made the Marx Brothers rich. The next three years saw them have two more smash hit successes on Broadway with *The Cocoanuts* (377 performances) and *Animal Crackers* (171 performances), both written by George S. Kaufman and Morrie Ryskind, who would become responsible for some of the Marx Brothers' most famous lines – apart from those that the siblings wrote or made up themselves of course. In their script for *The Cocoanuts*, Kaufman and Ryskind introduced a new character, someone for the boys to play against – a straight woman. This character was played by the actress Margaret Dumont, who went on to became a famous and essential figure in much of the Marx Brothers' future work.

The Marx Brothers were the toast of New York. Groucho's many years treading the boards had been worth it. He was a Broadway star. His dreams of fame, success and money in live theatre had been realized. It was time to move on.

THE MOVIES

By 1920 it had already become clear to Groucho and his brothers that vaudeville was in decline and that the new medium of film was what they should aim for next. Other leading comics such as Charlie Chaplin and Buster Keaton had already made the jump from stage to silent screen, and the Marx Brothers wanted to do the same.

Taking positive action, they each invested $1,000 and found another $2,000 from financiers, and produced two reels of film which they called *Humorisk*. Joe Swerling, who wrote jokes for Groucho, was the main source of the extra capital, and one of his relatives owned a theatre in the Bronx. He arranged for a preview of *Humorisk* to play there, but the audience response was so negative that the Marx Brothers realized they had made a serious error of judgement, and that if any Hollywood film producer should happen to see it, their celluloid dream would never be realized. The master reel was burned and although one copy was kept for many years, it had deteriorated beyond repair by the time anyone retrieved it. The crux of the problem was that *Humorisk* was silent and, whereas Charlie Chaplin and Buster Keaton were masters of silent comedy, the Marx Brothers' humour relied almost entirely on their talented use of the spoken word.

In 1928 the silent film gave way to talkies, the biggest revolution the film industry has known. Al Jolson's *The Jazz Singer* had opened the previous year with dialogue and songs, and was so successful that Hollywood producers were rushing around trying to sign up good script writers and actors who spoke good dialogue. The Marx Brothers had recently signed up with agents William Morris, who quickly realized that their clients were perfect for this new medium, and they looked around for an interested party. They approached Paramount Pictures and attempted to get the brothers a package deal of $75,000. The chief executive of Paramount, Adolph Zucker, felt this was too large a sum to pay for the services of an unknown quantity, but he fell short of flatly refusing to talk about it further. A meeting was set up between Adolph Zucker, the William Morris Agency and Chico Marx. Chico, the inveterate gambler, played his hand perfectly with Adolph Zucker, succeeding in getting him to agree to make a film of *The Cocoanuts*, and also squeezing $25,000 extra, on top of the original $75,000 they had asked for. Furthermore he had also secured them a five-film deal.

Paramount Pictures had the Marx Brothers filming in Long Island during the daytime, while they performed *Animal Crackers* in the theatre at night. They were given a day off on Wednesdays to do their matinee performance. It was hard work, but the rewards were enormous and the years of performing *The Cocoanuts* on stage meant their performance and timing was polished and professional. Irving Berlin wrote the score, and although Groucho drove the directors mad with his constant ad-libbing, they were happy with the end result. So was Minnie Marx, who attended the premiere in New York City's Rialto Theatre and was able to see her boys become real movie stars before her very eyes. Then, on 14 September 1929, their inspirational mother died, aged sixty-five, which dealt the brothers a devastating blow.

In October that year both Harpo and Groucho suffered another disaster when the New York stock market crashed, and they both lost most of their savings which they had carefully been investing. It was a catastrophe. Groucho had not only lost his fortune but was heavily in debt too, having borrowed money to shore up his investments.

He was so stunned by events that he couldn't bring himself to get ready for his appearance on stage that evening, but just sat in his dressing room, brooding. Fortunately Chico came into the room and patted him on the back saying, 'Well, Grouch – that'll teach you to save your money. Now you're a pauper, just like your brother Chico… Don't let it get you down, Grouch. I've been in debt all my life. You'd be surprised at how easy it is to live without money – once you get used to it. I don't even have insomnia. I sleep like a baby... Look at it this way, Grouch. You lose your money in the market. I toss mine away on dames and gambling. Who has the most fun?'

The loss of his mother, followed by the loss of his investments proved a lot for Groucho to deal with, and led him to suffer from insomnia, a problem that plagued him for the rest of his life. While touring, Groucho spent some of the next few months turning his various magazine essays into a full-length book called *Beds* which was published in autumn 1930.

Fortunately, the Marx Brothers' popularity ensured them plenty of work to recoup some of their stock market losses, and they embraced it wholeheartedly in an attempt to forget their troubles. They went back to the studio and made their second film, *Animal Crackers*, which opened in August 1930. Despite the fact that their first two films were very 'stagey', as they had both been more or less transferred directly from stage to screen, the Marx Brothers' obvious talent showed through, and the boys from New York were poised to conquer Hollywood. But prior to embarking on their Hollywood experience, the brothers took up the offer of a six-week engagement in a London vaudeville theatre at the end of the year.

> How would I describe Hollywood?
> I love it! That'd be my only
> description of it. It's the
> only place that I'm happy in.

The Marx family had much fun in London. Based at the Savoy Hotel, the wives went shopping in the daytime while Groucho took his son sightseeing. They were removed from the House of Commons when Groucho took to his feet in the middle of a debate between the Prime Minister and the Leader of the Opposition and loudly sang 'When Irish Eyes Are Smiling'. He bought a football from Harrods and he and Arthur played football every day in Hyde Park. One afternoon an officious policeman told them to desist, that they weren't allowed to 'use the Queen's grazing ground for athletic endeavour.' 'The Queen's grazing ground!' repeated Groucho in astonishment. 'What's the matter with the food at Buckingham Palace that she has to come out here and eat grass?'

The Marx Brothers' reputations preceded them, and

everyone in London society wanted to meet them. On their nights off they went to cocktail parties and dinners with many famous people including some of Groucho's favourite authors. He met T. S. Eliot and became very good friends with the poet, corresponding with him regularly right up until Eliot's death in 1965.

After the success of their shows in London and Paris in early 1931, the Marx Brothers were eager to return to the United States and Groucho booked their passage on the fastest transatlantic ship available. On their arrival at New York harbour, they were presented with customs questionnaires to fill in. Groucho completed the form as follows:

Name: **Julius H. Marx**
Address: **21 Lincoln Road, Great Neck, L.I.**
Born: **Yes**
Hair: **Not much**
Occupation: **Smuggler**
List of items purchased out of the United States,
where bought, and the purchase price:
Wouldn't you like to know?

The customs officers on duty at the time were unable to see the funny side of Groucho's prank and so a thorough examination of the contents of all their luggage ensued. The ultimate humiliation came when the whole party was strip-searched, before officers eventually released them.

In 1931 the Marx Brothers moved en masse to California, where they settled themselves conveniently in and around Hollywood. They began work on a new film, *Monkey Business*, which was written specifically for the screen, and was to be one of their finest. Groucho, Chico,

Harpo and Zeppo played four stowaways on a luxury liner, trying to make it to New York. They each got themselves into dreadful scrapes with gangsters and bootleggers before smuggling themselves on shore, and ended up fighting a bunch of baddies in a barn.

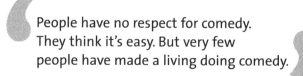

> People have no respect for comedy.
> They think it's easy. But very few
> people have made a living doing comedy.

At the time the craze was for gangster movies; James Cagney and Edward G. Robinson had succeeded in glamorizing the underworld, and it was a typical Marx Brothers move to make a film which sent up that milieu. The film starred Thelma Todd, who also appeared in their next film, *Horse Feathers*, and was the one woman other than Margaret Dumont to appear in more than one Marx Brothers' film. Thelma Todd was known to associate with gangsters in real life and met a tragic end when in 1935 she was found dead in her car in her garage. The circumstances were suspicious and it was commonly thought she had been murdered, though officially her death was recorded as being caused by carbon monoxide inhalation. By a strange coincidence, Groucho says the following lines to Thelma in *Monkey Business*: 'You're a woman who's been getting nothing but dirty breaks. Well, we can clean and tighten your brakes, but you'll have to stay in the garage all night.'

There were behind-the-scenes problems, however, largely between Groucho and one of the writers, S. J.

Perelman. He never forgave the Marx Brothers, Groucho in particular, for the rude treatment he was subjected to, and this mutual distrust and dislike was to last a lifetime. However, the film was a huge success, opening in October 1931 and breaking box-office records across America and Europe. *Monkey Business* turned the Marx Brothers into movie stars as rich and famous as any of their peers.

In March 1932, when the famous case of the 'Lindbergh baby kidnapping' occurred, the glamour of the gangster lifestyle was wiped out. America was shocked and horrified by the subsequent murder, and Groucho and his brothers knew they had to look for a new subject to debunk. *Horse Feathers* was the result, a story about a new college president who realizes that in order to save it, the college has to win the annual football game against a rival establishment. The film can also be seen as a metaphor for the world of big business – overly polite behaviour and hypocrisy masking a desire to win under any circumstances. *Horse Feathers* became another instant smash hit on opening later that year.

In May 1933, the Marx Brothers' father, Samuel 'Frenchy' Marx, died aged seventy-two, and the following month Zeppo and his wife, Marion, were the victims of an armed robbery. The brothers were having problems with Paramount Pictures, who were trying to wriggle out of part of their contract and so the brothers decided to terminate the deal. Meanwhile, despite all these blows, the Marx Brothers were busy filming *Duck Soup*.

Duck Soup is about a little country called Freedonia, which finds itself in deep trouble due to the fact that it is $20 million in debt. The immensely wealthy Mrs Teasdale is asked to come to the rescue, and she agrees on condition she can choose the next leader of the country – Groucho, playing Rufus T. Firefly. Sensing a good opportunity, the leader of a neighbouring country, Sylvania, decides he may be able to take Freedonia for himself, and sends two spies, Chico and Harpo, to look for evidence against the new leader. People change sides and all sorts of mayhem ensues, so Rufus T. Firefly declares war against Sylvania. After a great deal of havoc, Freedonia wins in the end, with the final scene showing Mrs Teasdale being pelted with fruit by all four Marx Brothers as she sings the national anthem with patriotic fervour.

The film sends up the lunacy of dictatorship and of war, and was well ahead of its time. At that moment the storm-clouds of war were gathering over Europe. It took almost forty years for *Duck Soup* to really come into its own: when the youth of the world took to the streets against American interference and aggression in Vietnam, *Duck Soup* was taken up by them along with Joseph Heller's book, *Catch 22*, as perfect anti-war statements. In the 1930s, however, with problems arising in the wider world and a new president, Franklin D. Roosevelt, in office in America, audiences were in the mood for patriotism, not for anarchic attacks on authority. Consequently, it was not as big a hit as their previous four films, but would later be regarded as a classic.

Fortunately for the Marx Brothers, Irving Thalberg at MGM was a big fan. He signed them up for a three-film deal, on the understanding that these films should have a bit more depth. Groucho was in his forties by this time, and so the brothers could not continue playing madcap youths forever. Irving Thalberg was married to the actress Norma Shearer, and her brother Douglas was MGM's sound man, and between them they were responsible for the next two Marx Brothers successes, *A Night at the Opera* and *A Day at the Races*.

> My guess is that there aren't a hundred top-flight professional comedians, male and female, in the whole world. They are a much rarer and far more valuable commodity than all the gold and precious stones in the world. But because we are laughed at, I don't think people really understand how essential we are to their sanity. If it weren't for the brief respite we give the world with our foolishness, the world would see mass suicide in numbers that compare favourably with the death-rate of the lemmings.

Premiered in 1935, *A Night at the Opera* had a different feel from the earlier films. Derived from a screenplay written specifically for the Marx Brothers by George S. Kaufman and Morrie Ryskind, the plot involved the brothers' attempts to give a couple of Italian opera singers a break in America. The crazy, chaotic style of the Marx Brothers was toned down, but the jokes and comedy moments still came in a steady stream. Douglas Shearer's sound production was a vast improvement on that which Paramount had achieved, and the director, Sam Wood, had even left enough space between lines for the audience to finish laughing without missing the next gag. MGM and the Marx Brothers had done it – they had a hit and it went on to gross around $5 million at the box office.

Filming on their next project, *A Day at the Races*, began in 1936, but less than two weeks later, Irving Thalberg, whom Groucho had come to trust and respect, died at the age of thirty-seven. Production stopped for a couple of months, but on resumption nothing went smoothly thereafter. Groucho wrote: 'After Thalberg's death, my interest in the movies waned. I continued to appear in them but my heart was in the Highlands. The fun had gone out of picture-making. I was like an old pug, still going through the motions, but now doing it solely for the money.' There were numerous rewrites, several scenes were shot in various different versions, and Louis B. Mayer, who owned MGM, made it clear that he was not a Marx Brothers fan – far from it, in fact. However, *A Day at the Races* was released in 1937, and it too was a huge success.

The film focuses on a wealthy hypochondriac patient, played by Margaret Dumont. She is about to leave the sanitarium to be treated by a certain Dr Hakenbush, thereby making the sanitarium bankrupt. The owner's assistant, in an effort to help, gets hold of the wrong Dr Hakenbush, played by Groucho, who is in fact a vet. Nearby there is a racecourse, run by a crook, where a jockey refuses to throw a race. The sanitarium owner knows Groucho is a vet but is determined to hang on to her wealthy patient, which all leads to a manic scene at the racecourse and a piece of classic Marx Brothers' entertainment.

By now, Gummo and Zeppo had both become agents, reducing the remaining acting Marx Brothers to a threesome: Groucho, Chico and Harpo. They were still contracted to MGM but were having difficulty in finding the next project. In the end Zeppo found it for them. *Room Service* had been a successful play on Broadway and was about a team of producers facing financial problems while trying to put on a new show. The brothers' friend, Morrie Ryskind, agreed to adapt it for film, and Zeppo convinced RKO that it was an opportunity not to be missed. RKO agreed, and MGM loaned out the brothers for the project. The film was released in 1938, but was only moderately successful.

In the spring of 1939, MGM were beginning work on the next Marx Brothers movie, *At the Circus*. It was the first film they had done for MGM without the support of Irving Thalberg. The world outside of America went to war that year, and some of the dismay that was felt generally about this spilled over into the entertainment business: fast-moving, joke-cracking films were beginning to lose popularity. *At the Circus* was followed by *Go West* in 1940 and *The Big Store* in 1941. These three films mark a downturn in the Marx Brothers' film careers. Although they were still funny, they were not making an impression on the audience, and so they decided to take a temporary break from film-making.

As America entered the war, both Groucho and Harpo promoted war bonds for the cause and went on tour to entertain the troops at bases all across America while they waited to be shipped out to fight. On a personal note, Groucho's marriage to Ruth had been in decline for some time, and their divorce was finalized in July 1942. Three years later, Groucho embarked upon his second marriage, to Kay Gorcey, and in 1946 his second daughter, Melinda, was born.

The Marx Brothers' pledge to give up filmwork appeared to be shortlived. Chico was always desperate for money, and Groucho was bored, so by 1946 an idea was mooted that they should make a film where they arrived in Casablanca, after the war, and have a confrontation with a group of Nazi war criminals, whom they would defeat, and call it *A Night in Casablanca*. The Bogart and Bergman film *Casablanca* had been one of the most successful films made during the war, and it seemed like a good idea to capitalize on its popularity.

However, the title of the Marx Brothers film caused a problem with Warner Brothers, who said they could not use the word 'Casablanca'. This enraged Groucho who fired off a series of wonderfully funny letters to their legal department on the subject: 'You claim you own "Casablanca" and that no one else can use that name without your permission. What about "Warner Brothers"? Do you own that, too? You probably have the right to use the name Warner, but what about "Brothers"? Professionally, we were brothers long before you were. We were touring the sticks as the Marx Brothers when Vitaphone was still a gleam in the inventor's eye, and even before us there had been other brothers – the Smith Brothers; the Brothers Karamazov, Dan Brothers, an outfielder with Detroit; and "Brother, Can You Spare A Dime?"'

A Night in Casablanca was released in May 1946, but although it was a great idea, it was not a big box-office success. Three months later Groucho went to film his first solo effort, *Copacabana*, with Carmen Miranda. It opened in 1947, and was a disaster. Later that year Groucho began to appear on his radio quiz show, *You Bet Your Life*, which was to provide yet another career for him.

In 1949 Harpo persuaded both Groucho and Chico to have one more turn together in a film called *Love Happy*, which would be the very last film they made together. It was released in 1950 and its primary claims to fame are that Marilyn Monroe has a tiny part in it and that it was one of the first films to use product placement. The film's producer, Lester Cowan, received extra funding from Kool cigarettes, Bulova watches and Mobil Oil, and their famous logos are shown amongst the enormous neon signs of Times Square, New York, while Harpo is being chased across the rooftops. *Love Happy* proved to be an unhappy working experience for the Marx Brothers; Groucho loathed being in it and hated the film itself. He did enjoy working with Marilyn Monroe, however.

The Marx Brothers had had a great film career; it had kept them together in the public eye for twenty years and given them their unique and unassailable place in the history of cinema.

GROUCHO GOES SOLO

In the spring of 1947, several years before the Marx Brothers' oeuvre on celluloid was complete, Groucho had recorded a Walgreen Radio Special with Bob Hope. His ad-libbing abilities were noticed by a young man called John Guedel, who produced and packaged his own radio comedy show called *People Are Funny*. Guedel thought that Groucho's talents would be much better displayed if he were allowed a much looser rein, and that possibly he should do a show working with members of the public rather than other professional comedians. A show of this sort would have the added bonus of being much less expensive to make than *People Are Funny* as he would not have to pay appearance fees to celebrities. He talked to Groucho about his idea, and told him he would like him to think about becoming the quizmaster for a new programme he was trying to put together.

Initially, Groucho was somewhat reluctant. He had had four disasters on radio, and wondered what could make this new programme more successful than the others. However, the film-making process had also started to bother him. As he slept so badly, he hated having to get up early and rush off to some film studio to be made up ready for work. It was an aspect of film-making that Groucho had grown to hate, when '…a bald-headed make-up man with halitosis slaps a cold wet sponge on my map and applies what he calls Max Factor pancake.'

Guedel went to see the president of the Elgin-American Compact Company, who was very much in favour, as he had seen and loved the Marx Brothers' show *The Cocoanuts* back in the 1920s. Having secured a sponsor, Guedel was then able to sell the show, called *You Bet Your Life*, to the American Broadcasting Company, and the first programme was broadcast in October 1947. Apart from a minor problem early on, when Groucho flatly refused to wear his usual uniform of frock-coat and painted moustache, the preparations went smoothly enough. Co-director Bernie Smith suggested that perhaps Groucho could grow a moustache of his own, and Groucho agreed to that quite happily. He was, after all, going to be in front of a radio audience, and he wanted to underline his performance as that of Groucho Marx the individual, rather than as a member of the Marx Brothers.

The format of the programme was based on John Guedel's previous show: there would be two carefully picked contestants at a time, who had to answer questions in one of four categories. There were cash prizes of $70, $80, $90 and $100. Each pair was allowed one answer in each category and their winnings rose according to the amount of correct answers. The pair that won the most money on each show were asked one final bonus question – worth another $100 – by a wooden duck dressed in spectacles and moustache, which suddenly appeared from above.

The first programme began with Groucho being introduced to the audience and saying, 'Folks, this is just as new to me as it is to you. I've never done one of these shows before. I only came on tonight because I heard they were giving away one thousand dollars in cash. Now I find out *I'm* the one who gives it away...' Groucho never met any of the contestants in advance, but they were carefully vetted by researchers before they were chosen.

A basic script was produced for each show, put together by one or more of the four writers involved, and Groucho's job was to ad-lib around it. The result was a very smooth, well-produced show, and the audience loved it. Groucho not only teased the contestants, but he also had a straight man to play to – George Fenneman started out by reading the commercials but soon became the show's 'male Margaret Dumont' as Groucho put it.

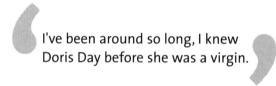

> I've been around so long, I knew
> Doris Day before she was a virgin.

In 1949 the highly successful *You Bet Your Life* moved over to CBS and reached sixth place in the radio ratings. Groucho's solo career bloomed, while keeping him in the public consciousness, and the show ran for three years before changing networks and being turned into a television programme.

An attempt at a writing partnership with Norman Krasna proved unsuccessful in 1948, when their Broadway production of *Time For Elizabeth* opened in September, but only ran for eight performances.

After finishing the filming of *Love Happy*, in 1950, Groucho was largely occupied with *You Bet Your Life*. Comedy shows were exceptionally popular and the networks were all competing madly with each other for them. Most of these shows had begun on NBC, but gradually CBS, by offering larger salaries plus the chance to work on television, the up-and-coming popular new medium, began to tempt many shows over to their network. CBS badly wanted *You Bet Your Life* to move over too and William S. Paley, who was the president of CBS at that time, became involved personally in the effort to achieve this.

One evening Paley arrived uninvited at Groucho's house in Beverly Hills. Groucho, Gummo and John Guedel were sitting around discussing the various options open to them. He asked if he could have a private word with Groucho and said to him, 'Look, you're a Jew and I'm a Jew. We should stick together. You can't afford to sign with NBC.' Groucho had always despised the 'we're all Jews together' approach, and in any case NBC was both owned and run by a Jewish man called David Sarnoff. Groucho let Paley know in no uncertain terms that he had no interest in such a conversation, and so the CBS President left.

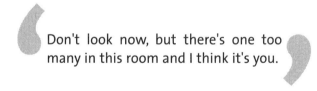

Don't look now, but there's one too many in this room and I think it's you.

Groucho then signed with NBC, and both he and Guedel, who packaged the programme, negotiated themselves a lucrative deal. Groucho was to receive $760,000 per year for ten years, plus $48,000 per week for the thirty-nine-week run of the show each year. Guedel also secured a ten-year deal with a separate thirty-nine-week salary on top. In 1950, the deal was worth a fortune – Groucho was making more money than he had ever dreamed of.

NBC wanted Groucho to go back to his most famous persona and wear the Hackenbush clothes and make-up, but he steadfastly refused, agreeing to wear a hairpiece only and keeping his own moustache.

Groucho's marriage to Kay had broken down, and divorce followed in May 1950. Initially, his ex-wife had custody of their six-year-old, Melinda, but as Groucho had his daughter with him most of the time, he eventually won back custody. Melinda, who had taken part in several episodes of *You Bet Your Life* when it was performed in front of a live audience and recorded for radio, was prepped to make more appearances when the show transferred to television. Groucho made no concessions to her, expecting her to be as professional as he was.

Melinda's job was, effectively, to let the audience know that underneath the sharp-tongued, quick-witted and rather frightening exterior of Groucho, lurked an old softie who dearly loved his little girl. Years later Groucho said about this, 'Being your typical proud and doting father, I wanted to show off her gifts to the world. I might have been a bit smug about her talent, which was obviously inherited. I was tickled with the idea that a third generation of performing Marxes was being introduced to the public.' Melinda had to sing and dance on the show, and she hated the pressure that was attached to it. She loved singing and dancing, as do most small girls but, as she said later, 'It became very intense and uncomfortable and something I didn't want to do at all.' In his enthusiasm for her developing career, her father had completely failed to notice her anxiety.

As well as the television show, Groucho managed to fit

in plenty of other work too. He had a cameo part in the 1950 film *Mr Music*, which starred Bing Crosby, and in 1951 landed a comic part in a film co-starring Frank Sinatra and Jane Russell called *Double Dynamite*. Frank Sinatra was a big star, and as such, took advantage of his status, often arriving on set very late, making the rest of the cast wait for his arrival. Groucho was unimpressed by either Sinatra's Mafia connections or his star status, and soon put him in his place: 'I believe in being on time to work. The next time you show up late, you'd better be prepared to act for two because I won't be there!' This little outburst did the trick, and Sinatra never kept the cast waiting again.

> Man is the only rat who's always looking for cheesecake instead of cheese.

Groucho was a busy man: he quickly followed *Double Dynamite* with another film for RKO entitled *A Girl in Every Port* in 1952, and he also began pushing Melinda on to other people's shows, for $2,500 an appearance. He was earning vast amounts of money for *You Bet Your Life*, which by now had become a household name. The advertisement that was run for the show said it all: 'One Man In A Chair Has Drawn More Viewers Over The Last Six Years Than Any Other Attraction On Television.'

The 'Reds Under The Bed' McCarthy hearings were in progress in the early 1950s, and Groucho did his best to keep NBC and the show's sponsors happy. When Jerry

Fielding, musical director of *You Bet Your Life*, had been subpoenaed backstage at the show, Groucho had made light of the situation at the time. After Fielding chose to claim the Fifth Amendment when he testified, however, he was instantly dropped from the show, becoming *persona non grata*. No one would answer his phone calls, not even Groucho. But twenty years later Groucho was to say of that affair, 'That I bowed to sponsors' demands is one of the greatest regrets of my life.'

Groucho had married his third wife, Eden, in July 1954, and was also busy appearing on other people's shows for a fee, and made a record of Bert Kalmar and Harry Ruby's dotty, surreal songs, which included gems such as, 'There's A Place Called Omaha, Nebraska'. He was rich, famous and much sought after. However, by the end of the 1950s he began to think that *You Bet Your Life* had more or less run out of steam, though it continued until 1961. He was sixty-seven years old, but dreaded the thought of not working. He and Eden decided to tour together in *Time For Elizabeth*, and they played to full or almost full houses for nearly three summer seasons.

In 1959, Groucho, Harpo and Chico got together again for yet another farewell performance, in a film called *The Story of Mankind*, although they did not appear in any scenes together. They also featured in a CBS half-hour theatre show called *The Incredible Jewel Robbery*. CBS was prevented from advertising Groucho's appearance in advance, because he was contracted to NBC. The show was a disaster; hardly anyone watched it and the notices were bad. A short while later another effort to kick-start a joint career for the three of them was arranged by Phil Rapp, who had written comedy routines for both George

Burns and Eddie Cantor. The show was due to be called *Deputy Seraph*, but they failed to complete the pilot show because Chico, aged seventy-two by now, was diagnosed with arteriosclerosis.

In 1961, Groucho was invited to play Ko-Ko, the Lord High Executioner in *The Mikado*, which was being sponsored on television by the Bell Telephone Company. He wrote to Norman Krasna, the co-author of *Time For Elizabeth*, about the job, saying, 'This is my revenge for the lousy phone service they've given me over the years.' In actual fact, he was thrilled to be doing it – he had always adored Gilbert and Sullivan, and was exceedingly knowledgeable about them and their work, and he rehearsed his part tirelessly to be quite sure that he did not let them down. Melinda was asked to play one of the 'Three Little Maids From School', which added to his pleasure. It was beautifully produced, and although the critics were less than kind to Groucho, the audience was impressed, the ratings were good and Bell Telephone were so delighted that they asked if he would star in *The Pirates of Penzance* the following season.

Groucho was seventy years old when he gave up the role of quizmaster on *You Bet Your Life*. He still wanted to work, though he realized that he could no longer do as much as he used to. A month after the last show, in 1961, Chico died in hospital. That night, Groucho took his son Arthur, and Arthur's wife Lois, out to dinner. Arthur remembers that for the first time in his life he saw Groucho drink four straight whiskies, and he and Lois had to help Groucho home.

Groucho settled down to put together his book *Memoirs of a Mangy Lover*, a collection of old articles and musings about life, and decided to appear in a television version of *Time For Elizabeth*. His wife was also given a part and it was screened, in colour, in 1964. Groucho did not see its transmission, however, as he and Eden were in England at the time. Groucho had accepted an invitation to host an English television programme called *The Celebrity Game* with panelists Kingsley Amis, Brian Epstein and Susan Hampshire.

> Age is not a particularly interesting subject. Anyone can get old. All you have to do is live long enough.

Back home once more, Groucho tried to interest various people in a variety of different projects. He knew his star status was fading, even invitations to appear on other people's shows were becoming less frequent. It was at this time, however, that he first met Woody Allen, a huge fan who became a friend, on Dick Cavett's *The Tonight Show*. None of his projects were being given proper consideration for production, but the unexpected death of Harpo in September 1964 overshadowed his ambitions, and he fell into a near-depressive state.

In 1965 Groucho managed a reunion with Margaret Dumont in a television show called *The Hollywood Palace*. The show was well received, but sadly Margaret Dumont died just a few days after they had finished recording. Depressed again, Groucho took off for London to host a comedy show called *Groucho*. It was unsuccessful, and thirteen weeks later Groucho was back in California. There he made a few television appearances, but for the most part stayed at home. He was not at all well, suffering from prostate problems and a chronic bladder condition that caused him considerable pain. He did accept a cameo part in an Otto Preminger film called *Skiddo*, which was released in 1968, but he regretted it almost instantly, realizing that the film was destined to be a failure.

Groucho had hit a very low period in his life, not only professionally but also domestically – he and Eden were experiencing marital difficulties, and early in January 1969 she left him.

GROUCHO'S LATER YEARS

After Eden's departure early in 1969, Groucho strove to beat his depression by involving himself once again with the world of show business. Arthur, his son, and his partner Bob Fisher were approached by the Broadway producer, Arthur Whitelaw who dreamed up the idea of a musical about the Marx Brothers, to be called *Minnie's Boys*, starring Shelley Winters as Minnie Marx. The show opened in March 1970 to quite poor reviews, despite input from Groucho himself on the opening night, and it closed in May after only sixty performances.

Groucho had a successful bladder operation in September, and on his recovery, threw himself into making plans for a big eightieth birthday bash. After the party, however, life reverted to normal and Groucho became downhearted again.

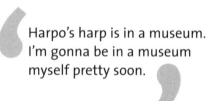

Harpo's harp is in a museum. I'm gonna be in a museum myself pretty soon.

It was at this time that Groucho got into trouble with the FBI. Magazines and newspapers continued to love him and he was still able to provide great copy for his quite frequent interviews. When an underground newspaper asked for his views on President Nixon he replied: '...I think the only hope this country has is Nixon's assassination.' Within forty-eight hours this quote was on wire services all over the world and Groucho was in serious hot water with the FBI. He responded to this as only he could, and put out a press statement saying, 'I deny everything, because I never tell the truth. I lie about everything I do or say – about men, women or any other sex.' The Nixon camp were not impressed. A singularly humourless bunch, they took steps to ensure that eighty-year-old Groucho was placed on FBI files as a potential threat to the life of the Chief Executive.

> Getting old isn't all that great...
> Now, getting younger...
> that would be something.

The anti-Vietnam war movement took Groucho to their hearts over his anarchic remark, but Arthur, by then aged fifty, was concerned that his father was losing his faculties, and needed a companion-cum-manager who could keep him out of trouble and look after him properly. The TV producer Jerry Davis invited Groucho to a dinner party, saying he had someone there he would like him to meet. It was Erin Fleming, and within a very short time she had completely changed Groucho's life.

Erin took over all Groucho's correspondence and became his close companion and manager. She was in her early thirties, and very ambitious, not just for herself but also for Groucho. She began suggesting to Groucho that he perform a show at Carnegie Hall. Initially, he was not wholly enthusiastic about the idea, but gradually he warmed to it. Erin convinced him that he could put on a top-flight show and he decided that with Erin at his side, and with Marvin Hamlisch to accompany him on the piano, he would give it a try.

 Look, I got a cheque. I'm still alive.

In 1972, Groucho and Erin gave the show a trial at Iowa State University, to gauge the audience reaction. The students loved it. At the time, the Marx Brothers' film *Duck Soup* was a big success all over again at campuses throughout the United States, it being a mockery of diplomacy at a time when American diplomacy had a bad name during the Vietnam War. Groucho's personal stock was high since his run-in with the FBI, so when he showed up wearing blue jeans the students gave him a terrific welcome.

Groucho and Erin were photographed walking through the campus grounds holding hands, and the image was published in *Life* magazine. With a lovely young woman at his side, his reputation was given a huge boost, and by the time they were ready for the Carnegie Hall show they were the talk of the town, and everybody who was anybody had bought tickets. In fact the hall was fully booked several weeks in advance.

 I'm as young as the day is long, and this has been a very short day.

May 6 1972 was a big night for Groucho. Dick Cavett introduced him to the star-studded audience and despite Groucho's obvious frailty, they laughed at his jokes and loved his performance. A & M Records recorded the show, and issued it as an LP entitled *An Evening With Groucho*. The record was a big success, and eighty-one-year-old Groucho found himself firmly back where he liked to be – in the public eye once more.

Groucho was back, and he was buzzing. Later that month he and Erin left for the Cannes Film Festival where he was awarded Commandeur dans l'Ordre des Arts et des Lettres. As the festival president placed the medal around his neck, Groucho joked, 'All the way from Beverly Hills for this! It's not even real gold.'

> I'm going to Iowa for an award. Then I'm appearing at Carnegie Hall, it's sold out. Then I'm sailing to France to be honoured by the French government. I'd give it all up for one erection.

An emissary arrived to see Groucho, sent from Buckingham Palace, asking if he would perform for the Queen at a Royal Command Performance. This appealed to him greatly, and he was about to accept when he was told that all the proceeds of these shows went to charity. He sent back his reply: 'Tell the Queen that Groucho doesn't work for nothing.' Erin thought that this was a typical Groucho-ism, but some of Groucho's friends thought it was a sign that he was losing it. Erin responded by doing an interview with Groucho for *Vogue*, in which he appeared to be as bright and sparky as ever.

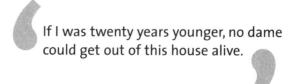

If I was twenty years younger, no dame could get out of this house alive.

In August, not long after their return from Cannes, Groucho and Erin went to San Francisco to do another show. This was another great success, and critics and fans who had also seen the two previous shows all agreed that this was the best one yet. Groucho received four standing ovations and was delighted with his reception. Erin had booked him to perform in Los Angeles the next month, but on 13 September, Groucho had a minor stroke. He seemed to recover well, but was left with a slight speech defect. Erin had to postpone the Los Angeles show, however, and did so by telling the press that Groucho was suffering from exhaustion and depression following the murder of the Israeli athletes at the Olympic Games in Munich earlier that month.

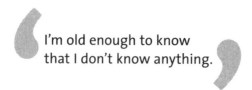

I'm old enough to know that I don't know anything.

Erin managed to persuade Groucho to sign various legal documents during this period, including one which confirmed her employment as Groucho's personal manager, and awarded her 25 per cent of all his net earnings. Then she finally booked the Los Angeles venue, the Taper Forum, for the concert. Groucho was old and ill, and the concert was a total disaster. There was a videotape made of the performance, but Groucho was so debilitated and pathetic that it was never released. The *Los Angeles Times* tried to gloss over the affair as best it could, but did suggest that Groucho should retire. He never gave another concert again, but still appeared on talk shows. Arthur had written a book about him, entitled *Son of Groucho*, and with his father's endorsement, ensured that Groucho remained in the public eye.

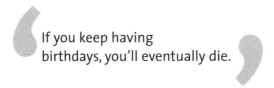

If you keep having birthdays, you'll eventually die.

Despite his failing health, Erin continued to produce new ideas of how to market Groucho. Boosting her own profile, she took a part in an avant-garde play, which Groucho went to see accompanied by Arthur and Lois. Groucho had been unaware that she would be playing her part half-naked, and was understandably quite shocked.

A few weeks later, Arthur rang his father to invite him to dinner at a trendy restaurant with Lois and himself. Groucho turned down the offer, but Arthur and Lois went anyway. While dining, they saw Erin enter the restaurant with a good-looking man. Sitting together in a booth, Erin's behaviour made it quite clear that this man was more than just a friend. Outraged, Lois approached the booth and poured a glass of cold water over Erin as she and Arthur left. Such a public incident could not be kept private for long, and after a while, Groucho heard about the upsetting news.

> I'm not interested in sex any more. I like to see a good-looking woman – that's as far as it goes. Sex is a god-damn nuisance when you get older. Women still accost me, mostly elderly ones. Younger ones know there's nothing going on.

Arthur had repeatedly made it plain that he was extremely suspicious of Erin's motives, but Erin was Groucho's adored companion, who had brought more excitement to his life than he had experienced in a long time, and he refused to accept his son's reservations. Instead, Groucho told Arthur that Lois had to apologize to Erin, and that if she did not do so, he would cut Arthur out of his will. With Arthur's full support, Lois refused to apologize, and so Groucho and his son ceased contact. Arthur felt that Groucho had been asked to choose between himself and Erin, and that Erin had won. At this point Groucho decided to work with a freelance writer called Richard J. Anobile, who suggested that Groucho should sit down with him and record his memories and thoughts about life. The book was to be called *The Marx Bros. Scrapbook.*

It included interviews with various people who had been important to Groucho throughout his life, previously unpublished photographs and Groucho's own words. When it appeared, it was not only full of basic mistakes, but also, as the critic Wilfred Sheed pointed out, 'sleazy breaches of trust'. Anobile responded by saying that Groucho not only knew that he should not say anything in the recorded interviews that he was not happy to see in print, but that also he had signed the author's copy saying, 'This is a wonderful book, Richard, thanks to you', and had offered to go on talk shows to help promote it. Groucho was a vulnerable old man, and had been exploited.

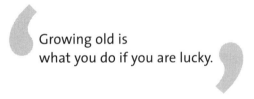

Growing old is
what you do if you are lucky.

Groucho contacted his lawyers when he realized his error of judgement, and began a legal action against the book's publisher and distributor, and against Penthouse Publications which was planning to publish a series of extracts from it. The legal action failed, however, because Groucho had signed a legally binding agreement with Anobile, which allowed him to print all the interviews in full.

Everything I did was a long time ago.

In 1973, with his health in decline, he went into hospital three times. During the year, after briefly making peace with Arthur, they had another disagreement. Arthur and his partner had been asked by Irwin Allen to write a television sitcom of the stage show, *Minnie's Boys*, but unknown to them, Arthur Whitelaw, who had produced the show on Broadway, had also become interested in doing a television version, and for safety had asked Erin if she would like to be the 'associate producer' if he clinched the deal. Groucho telephoned Arthur and told him to withdraw, to make way for Erin. Arthur pointed out that he and his partner actually owned the show, but Groucho said that since it was his life they had written about, he had every right to refuse to sign a deal with them.

On this occasion, Groucho decided to back down, and after inviting Arthur to see him, thrust a cheque for $100,000 at him. Arthur refused to accept it, saying, 'Is this a bribe so that I'll let Erin get the job?' 'No,' replied Groucho, 'You can have the pilot deal too.' Arthur then asked his father why he felt obliged to give him such a large amount of money, and Groucho replied, 'Because I don't want you to think your father's a son of a bitch!'

 I called my tailor, and a girl answered. I said, "This is Groucho Marx," and she said, "You're foolin' me. He's dead." And she was right.

Groucho's health was worsening daily, but in 1974, after much behind-the-scenes work by Erin, the American Academy of Motion Picture Arts and Sciences decided to award him an Oscar. At the ceremony Groucho accepted the award from Jack Lemmon and received a standing ovation from the assorted crowd of celebrities. Groucho made a speech thanking his brothers, his mother, Margaret Dumont and last, but certainly not least, Erin.

Animal Crackers, which had not been shown for many years due to copyright problems, was about to be re-released and Andy Marx, Arthur's eldest son, who had just graduated from the University of California at Los Angeles, was given the job of putting the old tapes of Groucho's show *You Bet Your Life* back into order so that they could be syndicated. So the Groucho business carried on thriving despite Groucho's own decline.

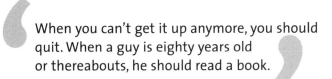

When you can't get it up anymore, you should quit. When a guy is eighty years old or thereabouts, he should read a book.

A few months after the Oscars, Arthur was advised by Groucho's accountants that, for the first time in his life, Groucho was spending more money than he was making. On hearing the news, Groucho's relationship with Arthur deteriorated further; Arthur left his father's house and did not speak to him again until 1976, the year before Groucho died.

Groucho: I'm still alive.
Woody Allen: How do we know that?
Groucho: I can tell when I get up in the morning.
If I don't get up, that means I'm dead.

Despite Groucho's frailty, Erin made sure that the Hollywood stars of the seventies came to visit him. She held various lunch and dinner parties, which resulted not only in Groucho being kept interested in life but also produced several books. One was written by Steven Stollier, an historian who had helped Erin get Universal Pictures to re-release *Animal Crackers*. Hector Arce wrote a history of Groucho's show, *You Bet Your Life,* and Lyn Erhard, a journalist who wrote under the name of Charlotte Chandler, charted Groucho's life in her book *Hello, I Must Be Going*. Groucho made good friends with the reporter, who even came to look after him for a while when Erin was away.

 A man's only as old as the woman he feels.

As Erin continued to push him hard, Groucho grew more tired. He still appeared on television chat shows occasionally, and he appeared on the Dick Cavett show, and as co-presenter of the Emmy Awards Show with Lucille Ball. Erin was happy with this state of affairs. A party was organized by Erin for Groucho's eighty-fifth birthday, and the mayor of Los Angeles formally proclaimed the day to be 'Groucho Marx Day'.

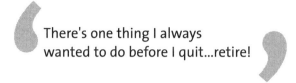

There's one thing I always wanted to do before I quit...retire!

Groucho performed for the crowd of 200 guests, and then, exhausted, retired to bed, telling them if they wanted to say goodbye, they would have to come to his bedside to do it. Two women got into bed with him, one on either side, and of course the resulting photograph made it into *People* magazine. Groucho was hitting the news yet again, and yet again a slew of invitations to various festivities arrived for them.

In answer to Jack Nicholson's 'How old are you, Grouch?' he raised his eyebrows and said, 'It's not how old I am, it's *how* I'm old.

Groucho's television appearances were dwindling by 1976, but Erin was still encouraging him to make personal appearances. At this time Erin's own behaviour towards Groucho was growing increasingly aggressive, and many of his friends and acquaintances found themselves thoroughly embarrassed as she lambasted him in front of them. Though his relationship with his children had been rocky in recent times, Erin suddenly decided it was time he made up with them and, obedient as always, though no doubt secretly relieved, he did. Erin began planning his eighty-sixth birthday party, to which his children were this time invited.

Relentless in her pursuit of publicity for Groucho, in 1977 Erin thought up an idea for a television special that featured various celebrities and entertainers exchanging comedic lines with Groucho at his home. Groucho's nurses noticed that he was becoming increasingly concerned about the event and that, as a result of the anxiety, he had stopped sleeping properly. He would get up far too early in the morning, saying he had lines to learn and a show to rehearse, even attempting to do a little dance routine. Very shortly after this, Groucho suffered a fall and broke his hip. This put paid to Erin's plans, and marked the end of Groucho's working life.

The hospital that treated him announced to the family that he had clearly suffered yet another undisclosed and untreated stroke. Groucho never recovered. He was dangerously ill, and was moved between a number of hospitals and nursing homes while his condition deteriorated.

 I wish to be cremated. One tenth of my ashes shall be given to my agent, as written in our contract.

In April 1977 Gummo died in Florida, but Groucho was not told, for fear that the news would be too much for him to take. Finally, on 19 August 1977, Groucho died of pneumonia. Arthur, his wife Lois and their son Andy were all present. Erin was in the corridor outside, in tears.

A performer from the age of fifteen, Groucho Marx had entertained and delighted audiences for almost seventy years. His unique sense of humour and comedic genuis would be widely missed.

GROUCHO'S WOMEN

Wife No. 1: Ruth

On 4 February 1920 Groucho Marx married Ruth Johnson, a dancer whom his brother Zeppo had hired in Cleveland, Ohio, after his adagio dance partner in *Home Again* had resigned. Ruth Johnson was the daughter of a Swedish immigrant and had all the attributes that appealed to Groucho's fancy: she was a Scandinavian beauty, blonde and blue-eyed, with a neat little retroussée nose. Groucho noticed the new girl almost immediately, and one evening, just as he entered the theatre in which they were playing, he spied her reading a letter and went over to talk.

 Will you marry me? Do you have any money? Answer the second question first.

According to his son, Arthur, in his book *Son of Groucho*, Groucho 'wiggled his eyebrows at Zeppo's new partner and said, "What are you reading, Babe – a letter from your boyfriend?"' When Ruth shyly replied that she did not have a boyfriend, Groucho said, 'Then how would you like to marry me? I need a wife to carry my guitar.' And so saying, he put his guitar into her arms. She looked at him nervously for a second, then smiled and followed him to his dressing room.

Groucho had always said that money was more important than love – an emotion that can vanish as quickly as it appears – but his three marriages were to women 'whose combined assets couldn't have kept one of them off welfare', and so evidently his heart ruled his head. He was very conscious of the importance of money, and decided not to rush into marriage immediately. During their engagement they worked together, travelled together, and ate together. Ruth, whose dance routine with Zeppo was flamboyant and sexy, was, however, a very respectable young woman. Marriage was what she had been offered and marriage was, what she would have. Groucho tried to save his money for a while in order to have enough to set them up properly when the time came.

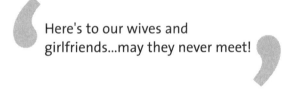

Here's to our wives and girlfriends...may they never meet!

By February 1920, when *Home Again* was playing at the McVicar Theatre in Chicago, Groucho and Ruth decided that the time was right for marriage. Ruth's mother was not amused. As a former member of numerous Christian churches, including Mormon and Seventh Day Adventist, she was not keen on the idea of a Jewish son-in-law. They also had trouble finding a minister who would marry them – not only because of their religious differences but also because they were in show business, a career that was still not considered to be respectable. Fortunately,

Groucho's best man, Jo Swerling, was able to find a Jewish Justice of the Peace who had been in vaudeville himself.

The wedding itself might have been a scene from a Marx Brothers show: Harpo hid behind a potted plant that he kept moving around the room to make it appear to be walking by itself, and Groucho kept the Justice on his toes throughout the ceremony with a lot of wisecracks, culminating with, when asked if he would 'take this woman to be your lawful wedded wife?' the swift retort, 'We've gone this far, we may as well go through with it.' After a quick celebratory dinner, Groucho and Ruth were back in the theatre giving another performance of *Home Again*.

In July 1921, Groucho became a father when Ruth gave birth to their first child, Arthur. He and his brothers had rented a house in Long Island, and were headlining for a chain of vaudeville houses around Manhattan, which enabled Groucho to spend plenty of time with Ruth and the baby. He even helped her to change and wash nappies, which was enlightened behaviour for any man in the 1920s.

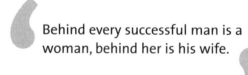

Behind every successful man is a woman, behind her is his wife.

When Ruth had recovered from the birth, she rejoined the act and for the next five years she, Groucho and Arthur were on the road together. At Groucho's insistence they stayed in cheap hotels and would not eat at expensive restaurants. They all shared a room, the baby either slept in a crib or a drawer. Without a nanny to look after Arthur, he was brought to the theatre with them. When this became impossible, Groucho persuaded a troupe of acrobats who were on the same bill, to babysit. The acrobats would do their turn, then rush to the hotel so that Groucho and Ruth could get to the theatre in time for their act. This worked for a while, but the acrobats couldn't resist practising as they looked after Arthur. This disturbed other guests in the hotel, who were vociferous in their complaints to the management. When they finally discovered the source of the noise, the management told Groucho that he would have to pay for five extra people and so the arrangement ceased.

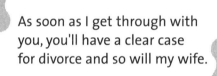

As soon as I get through with you, you'll have a clear case for divorce and so will my wife.

Ruth's constant clashes with Zeppo during their dance routine eventually produced a solution to the babysitting problem. Perhaps because he had been rejected by her in favour of his brother, Zeppo used to tease and torment her endlessly on stage, but she put up with his behaviour, being so determined to become a dance star. One day he swung Ruth off her feet so fiercely that she flew out of his grasp and landed on the kettle drum in the orchestra pit. Ruth was utterly humiliated, though unhurt, and demanded that Groucho do something about Zeppo.

When he refused, saying it was impossible to fire him as he was one of the four Marx Brothers, Ruth gave her husband an ultimatum – if Zeppo would not go then she would. This gave Groucho the chance to persuade Ruth to give up her career and become a full-time wife and mother. While accepting her role as wife and mother, Ruth felt resentment at her husband's disloyalty, and the fact that she had lost her chance to become a star.

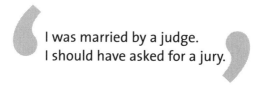

I was married by a judge.
I should have asked for a jury.

In 1924, after the huge success of *I'll Say She Is*, Groucho took the opportunity to buy a car and rent an apartment. He began to take the family out to dinner at smart restaurants, booking under the name of Jackson. This would irritate Ruth, who felt that finally they were in a situation where they ought to be able to reserve good tables in trendy places using the Marx name. Groucho refused to accept this point of view, believing that if he couldn't get a table using an ordinary name like Jackson, then the table wasn't worth having. He liked to preserve his privacy. Even so, his lifestyle changed: he began to have all his clothes tailored for him, and at Ruth's suggestion, hired a German couple to help around the house. After a while he actually felt financially secure enough to buy a house on Long Island, large enough to accommodate everyone with ease, just prior to the birth of his second child, Miriam, in 1927.

Groucho and Ruth were happy with their lot – fame and fortune coupled with two lovely children – but there were tensions lurking beneath the surface. Essentially, Groucho was a chauvinist. He loved Ruth because she was highly desirable, and also a good wife and mother, but he was unable to see women as equals to men. Ruth longed for affection from him, but outside the bedroom he used his humour to dominate and intimidate her. She was a woman with a limited sense of humour to begin with, particularly about herself, and she neither understood nor appreciated Groucho's witty remarks.

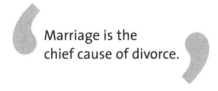

Marriage is the chief cause of divorce.

The couple were not well suited. Groucho was a self-sufficient man, and enjoyed being at home, reading books, playing his guitar and pottering about in the garden. Ruth, on the other hand, craved company and entertainment, wanting to go boating or to smart restaurants. The Marx Brothers were by now the darlings of Broadway, and were taken up by all the smart people such as Alexander Woollcott and Dorothy Parker. If Groucho didn't know what or whom was being talked about, he could always respond with a pun or a witticism, but Ruth felt completely out of her depth with his new friends. She tried hard to keep up, studied French, read all the latest books and took up bridge. She wanted to do everything 'properly' and had frequent rows with Groucho over his table manners. They also rowed about money; Groucho often accused Ruth of being a spendthrift, even when it was he who had bought half the goods in the most expensive delicatessen in town – the one at which he had forbidden her to shop. He won every time, of course, frequently reducing her to tears in front of delivery boys whom he would refuse to pay. He was a bully, even sending Ruth from the table to eat her dinner in the kitchen by herself when she had annoyed him.

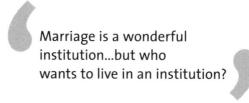

Marriage is a wonderful institution...but who wants to live in an institution?

Eventually, Ruth sought solace in alcohol. She found that a few sips of bootleg whisky gave her some confidence, and made it easier to cope with Groucho and his friends. This secret drinking soon became a habit and would ultimately lead to her downfall. In the meantime, however, it did give her the courage to demand that Groucho give her an allowance that was hers to spend exactly as she pleased. Groucho was not intrinsically mean, but after being brought up in financially difficult circumstances, he certainly had an obsession that he was spending more than he should and that they would all live to regret it.

Groucho was good with his children, if a little eccentric. He was constantly at odds with Ruth regarding their bad behaviour. When Ruth spanked Arthur for smoking cigarettes in the woodshed with a friend, for example,

Groucho was angry with her and told her she should use psychology and not physical force. If the children were caught doing something particularly bad, Groucho would send them to their rooms, telling them they could go without their dinner. This was the worst threat he could think of, having gone hungry himself so very often as a child, but rarely was the threat carried out; he would usually tell them they were free to leave just in time for supper. He was a kinder father than he was a husband.

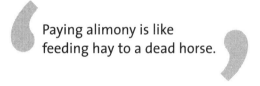

Paying alimony is like feeding hay to a dead horse.

In 1929 the Marx Brothers signed their film contract with Paramount Studios. Groucho was not at home as much as he had been, which gave Ruth more time to run her household in her own way. Without Ruth's knowledge, however, Groucho had invested all his savings in the stock market. He had taken tips from everyone, from the bellboy at the Boston Ritz to Max Gordon, producer of a string of Broadway hits. When the market crashed in October 1929, Groucho lost everything.

It was fortunate for Groucho that the Marx Brothers were still in great demand. He was still earning around $2,000 a week from *Animal Crackers* and their first movie, *The Cocoanuts,* had been released and had become an instant hit. All the brothers, except Zeppo, were on a percentage of the profits. So although Groucho had lost his savings, he was making more than enough to keep himself and his family in the style to which they had become accustomed, and was even able to start saving again. He did dismiss the couple who cooked and cleaned for them, and replaced them with a single maid, and he was careful not to leave on lights unnecessarily, or taps dripping.

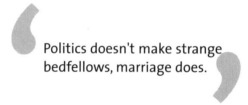

Politics doesn't make strange bedfellows, marriage does.

In December 1930 Groucho published a magazine piece called 'My Poor Wife' in which he said:

'For my part, I can only wish that my comedy during our married years had been easier for Ruth to bear. To be sure, she has never once complained. More often than not, in fact, she has encouraged me... For ten years she has been listening to my oft-repeated flippancies; she has heard me saying the same things again and again – serious things as well as skittish. Even all this – all that I have been telling you – Ruth has heard before. I'm sorry for my wife.'

Just before Christmas 1930, the Marx Brothers took up the offer of a six-week engagement in a London vaudeville theatre. Groucho and family, and their nanny, set sail for England on the liner *The Paris*. Groucho hated the sea passage. He was no sailor and was horrendously seasick – so much so that by the time the ship was passing the Statue of Liberty he had already turned green and taken to his bed. Ruth, however, had no such problem, and enjoyed life on board. She suspected that Groucho was exaggerating his suffering in order to avoid socializing, while she was happy to attend every event, and, as an ex-professional dancer, was particularly keen on the evening dinner dances. Groucho hated dancing:

> Dancing's only good if you're on the make for some broad and you need an excuse to keep your arm around her waist all evening. But once she's hooked you, and you've already seen her with her clothes off, what fun is there in just holding her waist?

Ruth had no difficulty finding willing partners; she was beautiful, a wonderful dancer, rich, and everyone knew who she was. Groucho was so sure of her that he happily let her dance into the small hours of the morning, while he stayed in their luxurious suite and read. On the night of the Captain's Ball, Ruth was thrilled to receive an invitation for them both to join the Captain at his table, but horrified when Groucho turned to the messenger and said, 'Go back and tell the Captain that this is a very bumpy trip and I don't want to eat with such a lousy driver.' Fortunately the Captain thought it was a joke, and sent the messenger back with a note saying he hoped Groucho would be as funny as that at the party. Groucho, somewhat flattered, accepted.

On the evening of the ball, they were in their cabin getting ready, when Ruth told Groucho that he had to wear a tuxedo. Groucho flatly refused and the row that ensued quickly degenerated into a terrible slanging match and ended with Groucho storming off to the children's dining room, slamming the door on Ruth as he went. Ruth was devastated and the children, who had been present throughout, were deeply upset. Realizing he had overstepped the mark, he sat and ate dinner with the children and the nanny, in almost total silence. As he heard the orchestra begin to play, he kissed the children goodnight and went into the main dining room, sitting himself down in his allotted seat, next to Ruth. She was so pleased to see him that she made no objection to the fact that he was wearing a pin-striped business suit or that he told the Captain that he had not been ill (the excuse Ruth had given for his absence) but that he had not wanted to wear a tuxedo and anyway, why wasn't the Captain wearing one when everyone else was? Ruth burst out laughing, and Groucho stood up, bowed to her, and said, 'Shall we dance?'

The husband who wants a happy marriage should learn to keep his mouth shut and his chequebook open.

Soon after their return, the Marx Brothers and their wives and families moved to Hollywood as they had planned before Minnie's death. Chico, Harpo and Zeppo all rented fabulous film-star-type homes, complete with swimming pools and tennis courts, but Groucho did not, much to Ruth's disgust. They lived in various rented houses that, according to Arthur, 'were about as spectacular-looking as the gardener's place on Chico's estate.' Eventually Groucho found a bargain property, a large, fourteen-roomed house built by someone who had just gone bankrupt. It lacked a swimming pool, and a tennis court, but had separate bedrooms for everyone, including Groucho and Ruth...

> When discovered by his wife, kissing the maid,
> Groucho said 'I was just whispering in her mouth.'

Harpo and Chico both lived nearby, and Groucho's family were able to use their facilities freely. They all became interested in tennis, largely because of Harpo's court. Arthur began having tennis lessons (he went on to become a nationally ranked player) and they all joined the Beverly Hills Tennis Club whose list of members was made up of virtually every star of the silver screen. Top tennis players began spending time there too, and it soon became the place to be. As the money rolled in, so the club smartened itself up, adding a dining room, a big bar area with a juke box, and a swimming pool complete with loungers draped with beautiful young starlets. Groucho loathed it and began to avoid it.

Why don't you go home to your wife? Better yet, I'll go home to your wife, and outside of the improvement, she won't notice any difference.

Ruth, as usual, had a completely opposing view, loving the glamour and fun she had there. The children were growing up, she had plenty of help in the house, and plenty of money too. She would arrive at around noon, play a little tennis, and then settle into the bar, dancing and drinking with the in-crowd of good-looking actors and tennis players who were more than happy to keep her company. Drinking helped her confidence, and helped her lose her inhibitions too, but her relationship with Groucho did not improve, as not only were they sleeping in separate bedrooms, but they also both kept their doors locked.

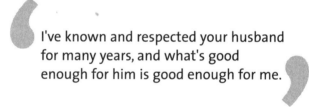

I've known and respected your husband for many years, and what's good enough for him is good enough for me.

Not yet forty years old, Ruth was determined to enjoy herself to the full while she was still beautiful. Groucho, at fifty, having spent years treading the boards every night, had no desire whatsoever to spend his evenings night-clubbing and drinking. A man of moderate habits, he preferred spending his evenings playing pool and talking with friends in his own home. Consequently, he and his wife began to spend less and less time together. Ruth had her own friends now, who liked to have the same kind of fun that she did. She tried to interest Groucho in ballroom dancing; he tried to interest her in Gilbert and Sullivan. They would fight and Groucho would tell Ruth that her trouble was having nothing to do all day while he was working. He believed that if she was busy during the day then she would be tired enough to spend her evenings at home with him. Ruth would then remind him that if he hadn't insisted on her leaving the show all those years ago, she would have been occupied as she would have become a famous dancer. Groucho would laugh and tell her how lucky she was that he supported her as she would have found it difficult to support herself with her small talent. At this Ruth would call him all sorts of names and storm out of the house.

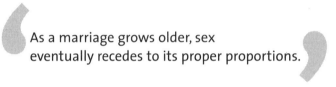

As a marriage grows older, sex eventually recedes to its proper proportions.

As their marriage deteriorated, Ruth's drinking worsened. She stayed away from home more often, and even stopped pretending to be interested in Arthur and Miriam's progress. Alcohol made Ruth angry and abusive, and Groucho would complain to the children that it was for their sake that he and Ruth had not yet separated.

After wrecking her car and breaking her leg on her late return from the tennis club for a dinner party they were meant to be giving for friends, Groucho finally had to accept that Ruth was an alcoholic and needed help.

Despite their terrible daily rows every day, Groucho was reluctant to break up the family through divorce. He was a reasonably moderate man in his habits and lifestyle, and although he sometimes had affairs with other women, they were just fleeting liaisons. Ruth and Groucho were no longer happy together, but despite her drinking and infidelity, he was not constantly cruel to her. He appreciated family life, remembering his own childhood with affection, as his parents had been as rich and generous with their love as they were poor in the material things of life.

> We all know that there is hardly a female alive who can resist the hand offered in marriage by some dolt eager to work his fingers to the bone for her. Making love to your wife is like shooting at sitting ducks.

Believing that the Marx Brothers' popularity was in decline, Groucho wanted to develop some of his own ideas, and decided to go to New York for a few days to find someone to produce a new play he had written. While there, he met a twenty-five-year-old woman named Karen Burke and they began having an affair. News travels fast in showbiz circles and soon Ruth had heard about the affair and went straight to New York to confront him. He admitted his infidelity, and they finally agreed to divorce. He dismissed the idea of marrying Karen when he discovered that she had slept with a great many other Broadway stars too.

With the decision to divorce made, Groucho and Ruth's relationship instantly improved, and they continued living under the same roof, while seeing other people, for a year or so, until the divorce was finalized in July 1942. Remembering his flippant suggestion of marriage to Ruth when he had first seen her in the theatre in Cleveland, Groucho declared it was the most costly remark that he had ever made. Ruth was awarded half of Groucho's money, the Chippendale dining room furniture and a sterling silver tea set. Groucho kept the house, and his daughter Miriam stayed there with him – Arthur had already left home – while Ruth moved into a small flat with her lover, a dance instructor.

> I believe that wives have a definite place in the home. They're invaluable as mothers, and also for keeping you informed as to when the lady next door gets a new car, a new fur stole, or is taken out dancing. Wives are people who feel that they don't dance enough.

After almost twenty-five years, Groucho Marx's first marriage was over, but there were more to come.

Wife No. 2: Kay

Groucho was a man who, while having a jaundiced view of marriage, much preferred that state to being single. Being single was somehow too much trouble. He had to make an effort to phone his dates up, pick them up and take them home again, make polite – or not so polite – conversation with their parents. After the divorce from Ruth, having had to part with half of a considerable fortune, he kept repeating that he would never marry again, but those who knew him well expected him to remarry in due course, despite his protestations – indeed he once said, 'I've tried being single, it doesn't work. You sit at a table, alone, eating.'

It is well known that young love is a temporary form of insanity and that the only cure for it is instant marriage.

Groucho's relationship with Karen Burke was short-lived and he followed that with another, equally brief affair with a twenty-seven-year-old divorcée named Virginia Schulberg. Virginia was an attractive and strong-minded woman who was not afraid of Groucho and would willingly stand up to him. Groucho told his son, Arthur, that he decided not to marry Virginia because of their age difference – he was fifty-one at the time – but in reality, he may well have thought her too independent for his liking, preferring his women to be of a more submissive nature.

Groucho met Catherine Marvis Gorcey while he was doing a radio show. She was twenty-four years old, pretty and blonde with a personality not dissimilar to that of Ruth's when he first met her. She was married to the actor Leo Gorcey, one of the *Dead End Kids*, but the marriage was already in serious difficulty when they met. Gorcey drank too much, and regularly used to beat Kay – as she was known – when he was drunk. Groucho's daughter Miriam who, at eighteen, still lived with Groucho in his new house in Westwood (he had sold the Beverly Hills house after the divorce, as it was too large for the two of them), acted as her father's assistant. She had met and made friends with Kay, and later introduced Kay to Groucho.

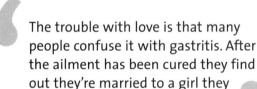

The trouble with love is that many people confuse it with gastritis. After the ailment has been cured they find out they're married to a girl they wouldn't be caught dead with.

Gorcey's threats against Kay increased after she had left him and filed for divorce, and she was really frightened of what he might do to her. Miriam persuaded Kay to ask Groucho for help, and Groucho, unable to turn down a pretty damsel in distress, suggested that she move into the house with himself and Miriam, where she would have some level of protection.

In 1945 Groucho married Kay as soon as she was free of Gorcey. He wrote to Arthur, stationed at the Coast Guard Headquarters in Tacloban, the Philippines, in the Entertainment Unit, jokingly saying, 'I'm going to marry Kay Gorcey on your birthday, July 21. This is in deference to you, and the fact that you can't be here to attend the nuptials, as they'd phrase it in the society section of the newspaper. However, I'm sure the war will be over by my third marriage, so you will be able to attend that one.'

 Until you have brushed a woman's cheek with your trembling lips and brushed your shoes with your wife's new guest towel, you know nothing about love – or your wife.

Groucho was very fond of Kay, despite being worried about their considerable age difference, and she was madly in love with him. The downside of their marriage was that Miriam was devastated by what she saw as betrayal by both her father and her friend. She decided to leave California, and enrolled in a women's college in Vermont, as far away from him as she could manage.

Despite parting on bad terms, Groucho and Miriam exchanged a number of letters, and their differences were soon resolved, and father and daughter were friends once again. He wrote of Kay that, 'We're getting along fine these days. She seems more sure of herself and certainly is trying hard to make me happy as well. You know I'm a peculiar individual and very trying, so if she can please me, she will be doing quite a job.'

In August 1946 Groucho became a father for the third time. He and Kay had a daughter whom they named Melinda. Groucho was thrilled with the new baby and wrote to Miriam saying, 'She's a remarkably good baby and rarely cries even when she's hungry. She's beginning to like her bath and kicks her feet. Last night I gave her her bottle and she makes the damnedest noise when she sucks the milk. It sounds exactly like a rusty farm gate and my hunch is she's going to be a very determined young lady – as God knows all of them are…'

When a man first gets married, he's always the first one in bed. Because he wants to warm the bed for his bride. And after five years, he's still in bed first. But for different reasons. He wants to get out of winding the clock, turning off the lights, and seeing to it that the maid is covered.

Despite the arrival of Melinda, the other women in Groucho's life were still causing him problems. Miriam's relationship with Kay remained strained, and in June 1947 Groucho wrote to Miriam asking her to begin writing to her and be friendly towards her again as Kay had told him that Miriam was only nice to her when she wanted something and that otherwise treated her with, 'studied contempt'. He told Miriam that apart from Kay's jealousy she was easy to get along with, and that he could imagine only too clearly that seriously bad feelings between the pair of them could lead to yet another divorce, something he did not want to experience again. He agreed with Miriam that Kay's jealousy stemmed from her insecurity, and that he kept having to reassure her that he wasn't going to 'run off with a new dame the minute one gives me the eye.'

> Marriage is a very boring thing after a while. The average couple, after they've been married for a few years, unless there are children to talk about, have very little to say to each other.

At the same time, Groucho was also concerned about Ruth, who was living in a very smart apartment on Wilshire Boulevard, drinking herself to death. She refused to stay in a sanatorium; the psychiatrists said she was a hopeless case, and as she would not admit she was a drunk, Alcoholics Anonymous wouldn't help her. Arthur and Miriam kept Groucho informed about Ruth and naturally he was concerned. However, she also kept ringing Groucho and asking him for more money, in spite of the vast sum she had received from their divorce.

Groucho, Kay and Melinda continued to live together reasonably happily for the next couple of years. Groucho was working, but without the kind of wild success that he had experienced with his brothers. Kay continued to be jealous and occasionally hysterical, and had frequent temper tantrums. Groucho was a difficult man to live with, but he hated rows. The fact that they kept different hours did little to strengthen their relationship. Groucho complained that he might just as well be single, for when he was awake, she was asleep, and that when she was awake she was always washing her hair. He cracked several jokes around this time, while being interviewed for newspapers and magazines such as, 'The trouble with marriage is you have to marry a woman – the last person in the world you could possibly have anything in common with.' And he wrote this to his daughter: 'Most men are just putty moulded the way their wives wish. I think that the great wars are the ones fought between the sexes, not between nations. I honestly believe that men and women dislike each other and only go around together for sexual reasons. If it weren't for that I think men would avoid women as though they were a plague.' If this was Groucho's true philosophy, it may explain why he was not a very successful husband.

Gradually the differences in their personalities forced them apart. The marriage ended following an incident over dinner one night. Kay was furious with Groucho because he wanted Miriam to spend her summer holidays with them, at home in California. Kay threw a fully loaded gravy boat at him, an act that signified the end. They were both fond of each other, but they just couldn't live together any more. Largely because they had signed a pre-nuptial agreement, Groucho was able to come to an amicable divorce settlement with Kay, who moved into an apartment on her own with the baby and the nanny. Kay was given custody of Melinda, though as she was travelling and working away from home, Melinda would stay with Groucho most of the time. He was able to keep the house they had lived in together, and three years later, citing Kay's 'illness' as cause for the change, he secured full custody of Melinda too. In reality, her 'illness' was alcoholism – after the split she had sought refuge in the bottle.

> I married women because they were pretty, and that's not the reason to marry a woman. You get fooled by their looks. They weren't stupid, but they weren't Einsteins either. It's better to choose brains. Beauty fades. I don't think most men are satisfied with their wives. I think most of them are looking around for another piece of tail. *Cherchez la femme*. It's the story of man's life. It's very difficult for a man to be true to only one woman for a whole lifetime.

Groucho stayed in close touch with Kay to begin with, but he was determined not to marry again. Twice was enough.

Wife No. 3: Eden

Shortly after his divorce from Kay in May 1950, Groucho's career took a turn for the better after becoming quizmaster on the radio show, *You Bet Your Life*, in which his form of off-the-cuff rudery was a huge hit with the audience. The radio show transferred to television early in the 1950s and was even more successful than before. Once again, he was the talk of the town, and making more money than he ever had before.

 Man does not control his own fate. the women in his life do that for him.

Groucho may have passed his sixtieth birthday, but he showed no signs of cutting down on his women or work. He spent the next three years escorting all sorts of pretty young women, from starlets to escort girls. He met up with a twenty-one-year-old former model called Eden Hartford at this time and they started going out together. Eden's real name was Edna, and her sister was named Dee, a *Vogue* cover model who married Howard Hawks. Eden liked to gamble, and Groucho took her to Las Vegas for a week. He himself had no interest in gambling at all, but was quite happy to provide Eden with $10 per night to lose (and she did) on the tables.

They went on holiday to Europe together in the spring of 1954, and rumours began to fly in showbiz circles that Groucho was going to get married for the third time.

Groucho still strenuously denied ever intending to marry again, even to his own children, until in June he wrote to Miriam from Rome ending the letter with, 'One of these days Eden and I may get married. I would like to know how you and Arthur feel about it?' On 18 July 1954, he sent Miriam a telegram from Sun Valley that read, 'You now have a mother named Eden. Love from both – Padre.'

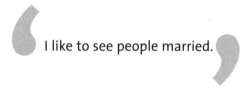

I like to see people married.

Surprisingly enough, Groucho and Eden got along well together. She was a relaxed person and paid no attention to Groucho's eccentricities. He himself was mellowing with age, and he not only had a larger income than ever before due to his television contract, but had also once again amassed a large amount of money in savings.

Eden persuaded Groucho to sell the house he had lived in with Kay and Melinda, and to have an expensive modern house built for her, complete with a round bedroom, a round bed and a sunken bath. They also bought a holiday home in Palm Springs – something completely new for Groucho, though Harpo, Gummo and Zeppo all lived there. He left her very free, probably realizing that a very young woman would be unlikely to stay with him for long if he kept his usual tight rein on her. He told Arthur that he wanted to be sure that she had a good time, and that even if she were to have an affair with someone else, he wouldn't care as long as he didn't know about it.

For the fourteen years that they were married, Groucho felt that he was as happy as he could expect to be. He retained his cynical view of marriage, however, and wrote in his book *Memoirs of a Mangy Lover*: 'Don't get me wrong. I am not suggesting that dogs will ever replace the fairest sex that blossoms in this great country of ours. That is something that every man will have to decide for himself. Personally I don't see why every man can't have a dog and a girl. But if you can afford only one, get a dog. For example, if your dog sees you playing with another dog, does he rush to his lawyer and bark that your marriage is on the rocks and that he wants 600 bones a month alimony, the good car and the little forty-thousand-dollar home that still has a nineteen-thousand-dollar mortgage on it?'

> **Questioner**: 'Is there anything in your life you would do differently?'
> **Groucho**: 'I wish I were young enough to make the same mistakes all over again.'
> **Questioner**: 'But isn't there something you would do if you had your life to live all over again?'
> **Groucho**: 'I'd try more positions.'

He thought Eden was happy too but, by the end of their marriage, no one else did. Eden confided in Arthur and his wife Lois one night at a party, after a number of dry martinis, 'I've waited this long. I might as well stick it out all the way.' However, 'all the way' was obviously a good deal too far for her and in 1969, when Eden was thirty-five and Groucho was seventy-nine, Eden walked out on Groucho, and filed for divorce, citing 'extreme cruelty' as the cause and asking for around $2 million, including property and monthly alimony payments, which she said was 50 per cent of the money he had made during their life together.

Groucho was stunned. He had known their marriage wasn't perfect but still believed that Eden loved him. He would rant and rave about how much she drank, how she didn't run the house properly, how she sided with Melinda against him, but that was just Groucho being Groucho. He certainly didn't consider that these domestic complaints could constitute grounds for divorce. In the end, she received about $1 million, and Groucho kept the house. Never a man to bear a grudge against an ex-wife, he started going out with her again just a few months after the divorce was settled. When one of Groucho's friends asked him how he could possibly date her again after what she had put him through, and wondered what he could find to talk to her about, Groucho said, 'There's a wealth of material – we talk over our old fights.'

Although the partnership with Eden was to be the last of Groucho's marriages, it was not to be the last of his important relationships.

Erin

In 1971, at the end of the summer, Groucho met a young Canadian woman named Erin Fleming at a dinner given by television producer Jerry Davis. She was an aspiring actress and had worked on the stage in New York. Her agent had suggested she might try to find some work in California and she had decided to see what Hollywood might have to offer her. Groucho and Erin got on very well and he quickly gave her a job as his secretary. When she told him that she had nowhere to live, he suggested that she move into a room in his house, where she could be on the spot to deal with his fan letters and business correspondence.

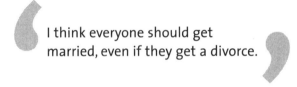

I think everyone should get married, even if they get a divorce.

Erin gave Groucho a whole new lease of life; her many detractors acknowledged that fact while also accusing her of abusing him both verbally and physically during his last years and of coveting his wealth. At the time, however, there was nothing obviously negative about Erin's influence, quite the reverse in fact. She refused Groucho's offer to put her on a salary to begin with, saying that board and lodging were enough. Groucho soon bought her first an apartment and then a small house nearby that had once belonged to Dorothy Parker. She was able to pick up several small parts in films thanks to being by Groucho's side so much of the time; Woody Allen, who held Groucho and his work in the very highest esteem, gave Erin a part in *Everything You Wanted To Know About Sex But Were Afraid To Ask*, and she was offered a small part in *Planet of the Apes* after Groucho and she had entertained the producer for a meal one day.

> *Bert Granet, comedy writer and Groucho's neighbour in Beverly Hills:*
> 'Of course his wives were well taken care of materially, but they were abandoned intellectually, and perhaps emotionally. Often they were ignored by a world of people who were only interested in knowing Groucho. Groucho's friends were always very important to him and Groucho loved to be in the company of writers. This might have left his wives feeling lonesome and left out sometimes.'

Most importantly, what Erin gave Groucho was hope for the future; indeed, a sense that despite his advancing years, he *had* a future. With Erin around, making plans for next year and the year after and the year after that, Groucho had new reasons to have fun. He trusted Erin's judgement and her influence spread to encompass not only business decisions, but how he should dress, and even the re-decorating and furnishing of his house. He began to spend more money than usual, enjoying himself immensely. He bought Erin a new car, and it was at this point that Arthur and his wife Lois stepped in.

Arthur, who had had a difficult relationship with his father since his teens, was convinced that Erin was dangerous, and that she was after his father's money. He had conducted some research into her background and was unhappy with what he had uncovered: previously, she had lived in an apartment block in Manhattan that also housed several writers and producers. On a couple of occasions she had presented herself at their front doors completely naked – her idea of an audition, apparently. Arthur had also discovered that she had written a letter to Bob Evans, as though it was from Groucho, complaining that he had not given her a part in one of his movies.

 Sex – this glorious experience that Mother Nature has improvised to keep us all on our toes and occasionally on our back.

Although Groucho was not happy about every aspect of Erin's behaviour, he loved her. After the row about the new car, he wrote to Arthur saying, 'No matter what you think of Erin Fleming I intend to keep her in my life. She's been very good to me, and I am very fond of her. The enclosed cheque [for $1,000] you can use to buy yourself a new car. Love, Padre.'

Erin persuaded Groucho to perform an ad-lib piece with clips from the old movies, along with some of his old songs, at Carnegie Hall in May 1972. Once he had decided to do it, he was desperate for it to be a grand success, which it was. Groucho's lengthy career was set to continue. Erin started booking him appearances in various other venues. However, later in the year Groucho suffered another stroke and, although he recovered quickly, it became clear, even to Erin, that in future, he would have to limit himself to guest appearances on talk shows.

While Groucho was still recovering in hospital, he signed Erin up as his executive producer, coordinator and secretary, for the tiny salary of $100 a week, but this was in addition to a generous percentage from his personal appearances and other work. Arthur in particular was growing increasingly worried about Erin's influence over Groucho. He became even more concerned when, just three weeks later, Groucho signed Erin up as his personal manager, for which she was to receive 25 per cent of all his earnings, and she proceeded to organize bookings for him to appear on various shows.

Aside from her attempts to find work for Groucho, she also worked hard to persuade various notables to push for an honorary Oscar award for Groucho, and after some months it was decided that they would indeed honour his success and talent.

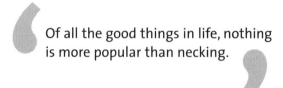

Of all the good things in life, nothing is more popular than necking.

At the Oscars ceremony, Jack Lemmon presented the award to Groucho for 'the brilliant activity and unequalled achievement of the Marx Brothers in the art of motion picture comedy'. In Groucho's acceptance speech he mentioned Harpo, Chico, his mother, Minnie, and Margaret Dumont, the actress who played the straight woman in many of the Marx Brothers movies. At the end of the speech he said, '...and last, I'd like to thank Erin Fleming, who makes my life worth living and who understands all my jokes.' This last remark lead to Erin receiving numerous letters from secretaries all over the world, thanking her for having given them a status boost.

> Most young women do not welcome promiscuous advances. (Either that, or my luck's been terrible.)

Erin knew that Groucho would not marry her, but she thought he might be able to adopt her. Whether for this reason or another, she began studying Judaism, and in due course converted to the Jewish religion. The ten Jewish men who formed the minyan – including actors Elliot Gould and George Segal – all wore white and Erin wore a long white suit too. Groucho took the ceremony rather less seriously than Erin. He told Lyn Erhard, who wrote under the name of Charlotte Chandler, 'Now, I'm converting. I'm becoming a Catholic and I'm changing my name to O'Hoolihan. Pat O'Hoolihan. The Reverend Pat O'Hoolihan.'

Erin was interested in all the traditions associated with Judaism, and took Groucho to the temple every Friday night. In 1975 Groucho told his lawyer to prepare adoption papers. This sparked another set of arguments within the family. Groucho remarked that Erin would be his only Jewish daughter – Judaism is passed through the female line, and Groucho had only married non-Jews. Martha Brooks, who had been Groucho's housekeeper for many years, and who grew to hate Erin, claimed that Groucho had said, in Erin's absence, 'I already have two daughters. What do I want with another one?' As a result, doctors were summoned to establish Groucho's state of mind. One found that his IQ had diminished so much that all he could do now was to respond to the most routine of questions and that he was terrified that Erin, on whom he had come to rely totally, would leave him. Another doctor found his mind to be sound but that physically he was in a bad way. Whatever conclusions were drawn, the subject of adoption was dropped, never to be raised again.

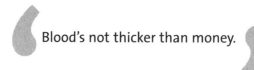

Blood's not thicker than money.

Erin encouraged various showbiz personalities to visit them for meals or drinks, partly to keep Groucho amused and partly to keep herself amused too. She was, after all, only in her thirties, and spending the vast majority of her time with an ailing old man. Jack Nicholson, Barbra Streisand and Bill Cosby all came by, as did Woody Allen.

During this period Erin had managed to turn Groucho against everyone whom she perceived as any sort of threat to her position in his life, be it family or friends. Even Martha Brooks, the housekeeper, could bear it no longer and resigned, despite being aware that Groucho had left money to her in his will, provided she was still working for him at the time of his death. People began to say that Erin was abusive to him, and even occasionally, physically so. One night, giving a dinner party at his home, Groucho failed to recall a funny story about A Night at the Opera that Erin wanted him to regale his guests with. Erin was apoplectic with rage, screaming, 'You stupid, senile old bastard!' in front of everyone. His guests were horrified and deeply embarrassed, but Groucho accepted the abuse.

> **Woody Allen:** Are you planning to do any more movies?
> **Groucho:** Erin's busy putting together a documentary about me. In the meantime I plan on dying.

Shortly after this, in 1977, Groucho suffered a fall, and fractured his hip. The hospital that treated him revealed he had suffered an earlier stroke that had been undisclosed and untreated, and as a result Arthur went to court to have himself appointed Groucho's legal guardian, with the Bank of America entrusted with overseeing Groucho's finances. A major scandal resulted, publicized across the Hollywood press. Erin became increasingly paranoid, and came to believe that Arthur had planted listening devices in the house, to try to get evidence of her abusing Groucho. She hired private detectives to look for these devices, but what they actually found was a bag full of syringes in a storm drain. When they brought the bag to Erin, she ordered them to bury it. Instead, they took it to the police, who had tests done on the syringes which showed they held traces of Nembutal, a prescription barbiturate.

> My guess is that, in the average home five years after the marriage takes place, there is more bickering and acrimonious debate over money than any other subject.

Groucho was so unwell by this time that he was barely aware of the fuss surrounding him. The detectives claimed that Erin had threatened to kill them both when they told her they had taken the syringes to the police. One of Groucho's nurses testified in court that Erin had given Groucho tranquilizers on at least one occasion, so that she could leave him and go out with her friends. Evidence was given of her verbal and physical abuse of him. Arthur claimed that Erin was a danger to Groucho's life.

In support of Erin, Zeppo believed that Groucho loved her and relied upon her, and that he would die if she were taken away from him. Groucho's doctor of twenty years told the court that Erin could 'stimulate and cajole' Groucho into a state of health and happiness that was beyond his own capacity as a doctor. Eventually the court appointed an old friend of Groucho's to be his legal guardian and when he gave up the position, Arthur's son, Andy, took over, with Groucho's consent.

In April 1977 Gummo died in Florida, but Groucho was not informed, for fear that it would be too much for him to bear. Erin was a constant visitor, and many of his old friends came to see him, although he wasn't too aware of what was going on around him. He was also reconciled with Arthur and Miriam.

In early July, Erin testified in the court case, denying everything that had been said about her, and telling the court that on a recent visit to the hospital, Groucho had said, 'You're the woman I love. I want you to stay with me.'

In spite of his failing health, Groucho still had comedic fight in him. His grandson Andy revealed that during his visit to Groucho in August, a nurse had arrived at Groucho's side with a thermometer in her hand:

Groucho: What do you want?
Nurse: We have to see if you have a temperature.
Groucho: Don't be silly. Everybody has a temperature.

Finally, on 19 August 1977, Groucho died of pneumonia. Shortly before his death Erin had told the press, 'Groucho's just having a nice little dream now. He's just going to have a nap and rest his eyes for the next several centuries. But he's never going to die. He told me.' No one will ever know the whole truth about their relationship, but there is no doubt that she brought excitement and fun back into Groucho's life at a time when he thought he had lost them forever. For each sorry tale of Erin screaming abuse at him, or threatening to slap him all the way to Pittsburgh if he didn't go and take a nap, there is another view: she gave him life, she forced him to fight, she refused to allow him to slip away into the depression and despair that he seemed destined to suffer without her by his side.

In 1983, during one of the many court battles that raged for years over Groucho's will, the judge ordered Erin to undergo a psychiatric evaluation. At that time she was found to be incoherent, angry and mentally ill. She disappeared into a world of mental hospitals and misery, and was spotted in the mid-1990s as a bag lady on the Santa Monica Boulevard.

THE WISE AND CRAZY WORDS OF GROUCHO

Groucho on Life

'Why should I care about posterity? What's posterity ever done for me?'

'No one is completely unhappy at the failure of his best friend.'

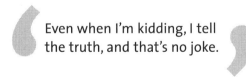

Even when I'm kidding, I tell the truth, and that's no joke.

'The Lord Alps those that Alps themselves.'

'I haven't worn a tie in years. I think it's silly to wear a tie. I'd like to go without pants.'

'The secret of success is honesty and fair dealing. If you can fake those, you've got it made.'

'There's only one way to find out if a man is honest...ask him. If he says "yes," you know he is a crook.'

'I must say that I find television very educational. The minute somebody turns it on, I go to the library and read a book.'

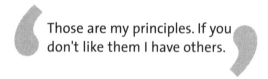

Those are my principles. If you don't like them I have others.

'Do you know what I say when I go to bed every night? "Unborn yesterday and dead tomorrow. Why fret about them if life be sweet?" Right now is the only moment there is.'

'It's a good idea not to live your life just to please others. You don't please yourself, and you'll end up not pleasing anyone else. But if you please yourself, maybe you'll please someone else.'

Groucho on Money

'Come back next Thursday with a specimen of your money.'

'What's a thousand dollars? Mere chicken feed. A poultry matter.'

'I made a killing on Wall Street a few years ago...I shot my broker.'

I worked myself up from nothing to a state of extreme poverty.

'Send two dozen roses to Room 424 and put "Emily, I love you" on the back of the bill.'

'How much am I paying you folks?'
'Five thousand a year. But we've never been paid!'
'Well in that case I'll raise it to eight thousand.'

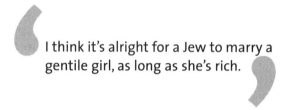

I think it's alright for a Jew to marry a gentile girl, as long as she's rich.

'In the old days, when people were poor they lived poor. Today, they live rich.'

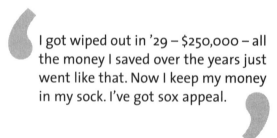

I got wiped out in '29 – $250,000 – all the money I saved over the years just went like that. Now I keep my money in my sock. I've got sox appeal.

'Just try to take a girl out when you're broke and see how far you get. I tried it one night and was back in bed at eight o'clock – alone ... with nothing to amuse me but a cold hot water bag.'

'Cleanliness may be next to godliness, but to my mind thriftiness would be closer. I consider myself one of the last survivors of a dying era. I'm the type that turns out the lights when I leave a room. I turn the water taps securely to make sure they don't drip. Although I have a cook, I go to the supermarket myself and pick out the food that she will eventually ruin.'

'I married three women, and between them they didn't have two cents.'

'I'm not available cheap. Free, maybe. Cheap, never.'

'When you're rich you don't have to eat everything on your plate. You don't have to look at the prices first when they give you a menu in a restaurant. You walk because you feel like walking. And they can't come and take away the piano.'

Groucho's son Arthur has made a number of observations on his father's attitude to money:

'He'd take ten people out to dinner at the most expensive restaurant in town, but he'd park the car two blocks away so he wouldn't have to tip the car attendant. He'd also leave his hat in the car so he wouldn't have to check it.'

'Even after all his successes, he can't make up his mind whether he is Aristotle Onassis or Scrooge.'

'His spending habits used to drive my mother right up the wall when she was married to him. One moment he'd be buying her a six-thousand-dollar mink coat or a diamond ring, the next moment he'd be bawling her out for not turning off the lights when she left the room.'

Groucho on Politics
and the Military

'Politics is the art of looking for trouble, finding it, misdiagnosing it and then misapplying the wrong remedies.'

'Military intelligence is a contradiction in terms.'

I think most people enter politics so that they can climb up on a platform and let other people look at them.

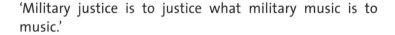

'Military justice is to justice what military music is to music.'

Groucho on Children

'I married your mother because I wanted children, imagine my disappointment when you came along.'

Woman: Oh, you like children?
Groucho: No, I like to make them.

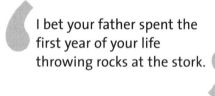

I bet your father spent the first year of your life throwing rocks at the stork.

'All children are cute. It's only after they grow up that the trouble starts.'

Groucho's Insults

'I never forget a face, but in your case I'll be glad to make an exception.'

'She got her good looks from her father. He's a plastic surgeon.'

'Do you think I could buy back my introduction to you?'

'Don't point that beard at me, it might go off.'

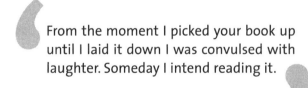

From the moment I picked your book up until I laid it down I was convulsed with laughter. Someday I intend reading it.

'He may look like an idiot and talk like an idiot but don't let that fool you. He really is an idiot.'

'I didn't like the play, but then I saw it under adverse conditions – the curtain was up.'

'I've had a perfectly wonderful evening. But this wasn't it.'

'Now there's a man with an open mind – you can feel the breeze from here!'

'You know, I could rent you out as a decoy for duck hunters'

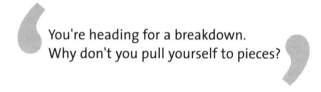

You're heading for a breakdown.
Why don't you pull yourself to pieces?

'You've got the brain of a four-year-old boy, and I'll bet he was glad to get rid of it.'

'Why don't you bore a hole into your head and let the sap run out?'

'Say! You haven't stopped talking since we got here! You must have been vaccinated with a phonograph needle!'

'Why, I'd horse-whip you if I had a horse.'

'She's afraid that if she leaves, she'll become the life of the party.'

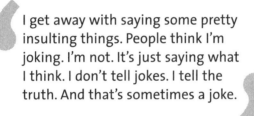

I get away with saying some pretty insulting things. People think I'm joking. I'm not. It's just saying what I think. I don't tell jokes. I tell the truth. And that's sometimes a joke.

Groucho's opinion of *Samson and Delilah*, starring Victor Mature and Hedy Lamarr: 'First picture I've seen in which the male lead has bigger tits than the female.'

Groucho once removed Greta Garbo's hat and said: 'Oh, excuse me, I thought you were a fellow I once knew in Pittsburgh.'

Groucho on Women

'Luckily, I was only interested in girls and myself, in that order.'

'The female is only about fifteen years removed from the jungle. This, however, is part of their charm, along with high heels, nylons, a bulging bra, and, even, white teeth.'

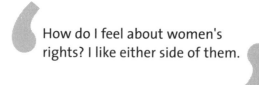

How do I feel about women's rights? I like either side of them.

'For a good year-round pet, there is nothing to compare with a simple, unpedigreed chorus girl.'

'Anyone who says he can see through women is missing a lot.'

'Remember, men, you are fighting for the lady's honour, which is probably more than she ever did.'

'We took pictures of the native girls, but they weren't developed. . . But we're going back next week.'

'Women should be obscene and not heard.'

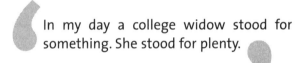

In my day a college widow stood for something. She stood for plenty.

'Why was I with her? She reminds me of you. In fact, she reminds me more of you than you do!'

'When I was young, I was crazy about girls. Especially if they wore silk stockings. In those days they had rumble seats in cars. Some philosopher said, "You can tell more about a girl watching her climb into a rumble seat than you can being married to her for twenty years".'

'I don't understand women. They're a different breed entirely than the male. There are a lot of things I don't understand about women, like why do girls always stand with one hand on their hip? Men don't do that. But I think a woman can be a wonderful companion. After all, my mother was one. I didn't find that out until a couple of years ago.'

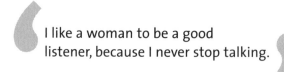

I like a woman to be a good listener, because I never stop talking.

'There's nothing more wonderful than a beautiful young woman.'

'Girls liked me. I don't mean like Clark Gable or Valentino, but when I was younger, women found me attractive. They found me funny. Certain kinds of women like a funny man.'

'It just always seemed to me that making love to a Jewish girl would be like making love to your sister.'

'Before I was married, I had a girl whose father was very rich in Portland. I could have married her, but I didn't like her behaviour in bed. She did everything. She was too sophisticated in bed. She knew too many tricks, and I didn't want a girl like that. I wanted a girl that was more feminine.'

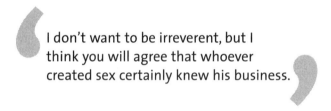

I don't want to be irreverent, but I think you will agree that whoever created sex certainly knew his business.

'Once at the Adolphus Hotel in Dallas I did it eight times in one night. I was nineteen.'

'Whoever called it necking was a poor judge of anatomy.'

'A man is the chaser of the two. It's nature. The woman is subconsciously the chaser, but the man is – a man is a man. And if there's an attractive girl, he'll make a play for her. I think that's wonderful.'

Questioner: Do you believe in computer dating?
Groucho: Only if the computers really love each other.

'Women are brighter than men.... I think generally women are morally far superior to men. Man is a beast. He wants to get laid. Women maybe would like to be promiscuous. But don't forget, if she's a mother with children, she's gonna defend those children. She wants those children. In those cases they are satisfied with what they have – the children and the husband. Women are miles ahead of a man. They can outfox him from the time they're born. From the moment a girl meets a man, she's casing his bankroll, arranging the furniture, and picking out names for the children.'

Terry Hamlisch (sister of Marvin Hamlisch, pianist and composer):
'When the lights go out at Groucho's house, it's every girl for herself.'

Groucho's Surrealism

'Whatever it is, I'm against it.'

'No, Groucho is not my real name. I'm breaking it in for a friend.'

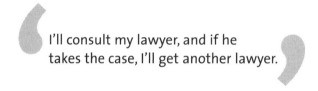

I'll consult my lawyer, and if he takes the case, I'll get another lawyer.

'Well, Art is Art, isn't it? Still, on the other hand, water is water! And East is East and West is West and if you take cranberries and stew them like apple sauce they taste much more like prunes than rhubarb does. Now, uh... Now you tell me what you know.'

'Either this man is dead or my watch has stopped.'

'Time flies like an arrow. Fruit flies like a banana.'

'Time wounds all heels.'

'I don't have a photograph, but you can have my footprints. They're upstairs in my socks.'

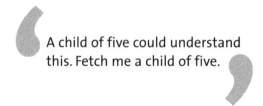

A child of five could understand this. Fetch me a child of five.

'I could dance with you till the cows come home, on second thought I'll dance with the cows till you come home.'

'I sent the club a wire stating, "Please accept my resignation. I don't care to belong to any club that will have me as a member".'

'You'd better beat it. You can leave in a taxi. If you can't get a taxi, you can leave in a huff. If that's too soon, you can leave in a minute and a huff.'

'I wish you'd keep my hands to yourself.'

'I write by ear. I tried writing with the typewriter, but I found it too unwieldy.'

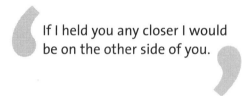

If I held you any closer I would be on the other side of you.

'It is better to have loft and lost than never to have loft at all.'

'Room service? Send up a larger room.'

'Outside of a dog, a book is man's best friend. Inside of a dog, it's too dark to read.'

 You go Uraguay and I'll go mine.

'Quote me as saying I was mis-quoted.'

COMMENTS ON GROUCHO
AND THE MARX BROTHERS

The pros...

'I loved his [Groucho's] lightning transitions of thought, his ability to detect pretentiousness and bombast, and his genius for disembowelling the spurious and hackneyed phrases that litter one's conversation.'

S. J. PERELMAN

'There was a natural inborn greatness in Groucho that defies close analysis as it does with any great artist. He is simply unique in the same way that Picasso or Stravinsky are and I believe his outrageous unsentimental disregard for order will be equally funny a thousand years from now. In addition to all this, he makes me laugh.'

WOODY ALLEN

'He taught us all how to be irreverent.'

GLORIA STUART (WIFE OF ARTHUR SHEEKMAN,
GROUCHO'S FRIEND, COLLABORATOR AND SCRIPTWRITER
OF SOME OF HIS RADIO SHOWS)

'The Marx Brothers were always doing crazy things. They didn't have to act in the films. Those films were about them. Nobody could follow them. And my style was equally impossible for following them. They created such pandemonium, no one was even listening to me because I worked quiet, like now, except I was even more quiet. It was pretty frustrating, but it was a big challenge. W. C. Fields said they were an impossible act to follow. But it really made me work, and I think, in the end, it helped me.

They used to break me up watching them before I went on , but you know, if you asked me what exactly it was that they said or did, I don't know. Even then, I don't think I could have told you exactly. You couldn't exactly explain the Marx Brothers. Also they never did it twice the same way. I always sort of envied the way they got up there and it seemed to come so easy, and they seemed to be having such a good time. In those days, I was trying to find the real Jack Benny. Now, I guess I understand that they were working too, though it looked like they were playing....

But Groucho was the genius. Groucho is a writer. That doesn't mean he wasn't great onstage, and he can be pretty funny off, too.'

JACK BENNY

'He was always putting himself out to make it more fun for everyone. It was a real pleasure to work with him. The one word that comes to mind when I remember working with him is "fun".'

MAUREEN O'SULLIVAN

'He walked over to his own picture on the chest on the day he got the Academy Award, and he slowly smiled and said, "Who is that jerk?" He really endeared himself to me, because he really knows that the thing I think people sometimes forget is the question, "So what?" We all try hard, we all struggle and strive, yet he's in a place where he sees the ups and downs, and he can keep his perspective on life and laugh at himself.'

TERRY HAMLISCH

'The only act I could never follow.'

W. C. FIELDS

'Je suis Marxiste, tendance Groucho.'

PARIS GRAFFITI IN 1968

... and the antis

'As far as their temperaments and their personalities were concerned, the Marx Brothers were capricious, tricky beyond endurance, altogether unreliable, and treacherous to a degree that would make Machiavelli absolutely kneel at their feet. They were also megalomaniacal to a degree which is impossible to describe.'

S. J. PERELMAN

'I never knew what bicarbonate of soda was until I wrote a Marx Brothers picture.'

HERMAN MANKIEWICZ

'*Cocoanuts* was a comedy; the Marx Brothers are comics; meeting them was a tragedy.'

GEORGE F. KAUFMAN

FILMOGRAPHY

and some of the great lines

The Cocoanuts, 1929
(script by George S. Kaufman, Morrie Ryskind)

'Be free, my friends. One for all and all for me – me for you and three for five and six for a quarter.'

Animal Crackers, 1930
(script by George S. Kaufman, Morrie Ryskind)

'What do you get an hour?'
'For playing we get ten dollars an hour.'
'What do you get for not playing?'
'Twelve dollars an hour. Now for rehearsing we make a special rate – fifteen dollars an hour.'
'And what do you get for not rehearsing?'
'You couldn't afford it. You see, if we don't rehearse, we don't play. And if we don't play, that runs into money.'
'How much would you want to run into an open manhole?'
'Just the cover charge.'
'Well, drop in some time.'
'Sewer.'
'Well, I guess we cleaned that up.'

Monkey Business, 1931
(script by S. J. Perelman, Will B. Johnstone,
   Arthur Sheekman)

'Sir, you have the advantage of me.'
'Not yet I haven't, but wait till I get you outside.'

Horse Feathers, 1932
(script by Bert Kalmar, Harry Ruby, S. J. Perelman,
   Will B. Johnstone)

'There's a man outside with a big moustache.'
'Tell him I've got one.'

Duck Soup, 1933
(script by Bert Kalmar, Harry Ruby,
   Arthur Sheekman, Nat Perrin)

'My husband is dead.'
'I'll bet he's just using that as an excuse.'
'I was with him to the end.'
'No wonder he passed away.'
'I held him in my arms and kissed him.'
'So it was murder!'

A Night at the Opera, 1935
(script by George S. Kaufman, Morrie Ryskind, Al Boasberg)

'Do they allow tipping on this boat?'
'Yes, sir.'
'Have you got two fives?'
'Oh, yes, sir.'
'Then you won't need the ten cents I was going to give you.'

A Day at the Races, 1937
(script by George Seaton, Robert Pirosh,
   George Oppenheimer)

'She looks like the healthiest woman I ever met.'
'You look like you never met a healthy woman.'

Room Service, 1938
(script by Morrie Ryskind from a play by John Murray)

At the Circus, 1939
(script by Irving Brecher)

'If you hadn't sent for me, I'd be at home now in a comfortable bed with a hot toddy.'
'Huh?'
'That's a drink!'

Go West, 1940
(script by Irving Brecher)

The Big Store, 1941
(script by Sid Kuller, Hal Fimburg, Ray Golden)

A Night in Casablanca, 1946
(script by Joseph Fields, Roland Kibbee, Frank Tashlin)

'Hey boss, you got a woman in there?'
'If I haven't, I've been wasting thirty minutes of valuable time.'

'I'm Beatrice Ryner. I stop at the hotel.'
'I'm Ronald Kornblow. I stop at nothing.'

Love Happy, 1950
(script by Ben Hecht, Frank Tashlin, Mac Benoff)

Groucho was also in the following films on his own:

Copacabana, 1947

Mr Music, 1950

Double Dynamite, 1951

A Girl in Every Port, 1952

Will Success Spoil Rock Hunter?, 1957

Skiddo, 1968

BIBLIOGRAPHY

Books written by Groucho

Beds, 1930

Many Happy Returns – An Unofficial Guide to Your Income Tax Problems, 1942

Groucho and Me – The autobiography of Groucho Marx, 1959

Memoirs of a Mangy Lover, 1963

The Groucho Letters – Letters from and to Groucho Marx, 1967

The Marx Bros. Scrapbook, 1973

The Groucho Phile – An Illustrated Life, 1976

Books written about Groucho

*Groucho Marx and Other Short Stories and Tall Tales –
Selected writings of Groucho Marx, 1997*
Edited by Robert S. Bader

*Why a Duck? – Visual and verbal gems from the Marx
Brothers' movies, 1972*
Introduction by Groucho Marx
Edited by Richard J. Anobile

*Love, Groucho – Letters from Groucho Marx to His
Daughter Miriam, 1997*
Edited by Miriam Marx Allen

Son of Groucho, 1972
Arthur Marx

Harpo Speaks!, 1992
Harpo Marx with Rowland Barber

Groucho – The Life and Times of Julius Henry Marx, 2001
Stefan Kanfer

Monkey Business – The Lives and Legends of The Marx Brothers, 1999
Simon Louvish

'Hello, I Must Be Going' – Groucho and His Friends, 1978
Charlotte Chandler

IN THE BEGINNING ...

There was

No Groucho

Then there was

Groucho

Then there was

The Larong Trio

Then there was

Lillian Foster and Master Marx

Then there was

Gus Edwards' Postal Telegraph Boys

Then there was

Ned Wayburn's Three Nightingales

Then there was

The Three Nightingales

Then there was

The Four Nightingales

Then (briefly) there was

The Six Mascots

Then there was

The Four Nightingales again

Then there was

The Three Marx Brothers
(Groucho, Harpo and Gummo)

Then there was

The Four Marx Brothers
(Groucho, Harpo, Gummo and Chico)

Then there was

The Four Marx Brothers
(Groucho, Harpo, Chico and Zeppo)

Then there was

The Three Marx Brothers
(Groucho, Harpo and Chico)

Then there was

Just Groucho

And then there was

No Groucho again

... But along the way he begat a lot of
laughs around the world.